KEEPER
Trial by Fire

By

Arline Fisher

Chapter One

2001

Jack Hamilton was basically a flunky for Oilco, working hard jobs in hard conditions with men much harder than himself. In the oil fields of West Texas Jack was getting quite an education, in the school of hard knocks. He never finished high school, and not because he was stupid, because he was smart, much too smart to be memorizing Shakespeare or conjugating sentences, skills he knew he'd never need. He had a near-genius level IQ, a fact his parents regretted sharing with him. His expectation of effortless success would plague him for the rest of his life. He also had an uncanny ability to fix almost anything mechanical.

"Go get Hamilton," was the refrain heard throughout the oil field. "He'll fix it." With the myriad number of moving parts on even one oil rig, Jack was kept running between more than three dozen rigs spread over twenty square miles. He had been a star football player in high school, his six-foot, four-inch frame towering over most of the other players, and he had spent enough time in the weight room to be heavily muscled, but working out on the rigs honed his muscles and his strength far beyond his high school physique. Naturally dark-complected with jet-black hair, the Texas sun turned his skin the color of burnished copper, making his dark blue eyes all the more dramatic.

Of course, he was relentlessly teased about his appearance. "Hey, Jack, you best stay up north here—you get too close to the border they'll snap you up and send you across the Rio Grande." He laughed it off, and other taunts as well. "No, there ain't no Mexicans his size. They'd throw his ass back over the wall." The laughing always stopped, however, when they saw how quickly Jack could size up a broken or jammed piece of equipment.

"Let me just give it a tweak," Jack would say. His 'tweaks' became legendary.

"I swear, that boy could tweak a Spam sandwich into a T-bone," one of the foremen said one day, watching Jack replace the gears in a grimy pump.

Jack derived some satisfaction out of fixing things and solving problems, but he was finally forced to admit that there was nothing satisfying about his life. He made good money, gave half his salary to his parents (after all, he still lived with them) and seemed to spend the rest on his truck or in the bars that catered to the roughnecks. One day was pretty much the same as the next, and Jack could see that would always be the case as long as he stayed in the oil fields.

He couldn't have expressed it to his friends or his family (and could easily imagine the ribbing he'd get if he tried), but he sensed he was destined for greatness or bound for glory. Pick either cliché, he thought to himself. There was more to life than fixing aging oil rigs in the barren west Texas landscape. Lost in his thoughts on the way to rig nine, he almost didn't hear the radio announcement.

"We interrupt our programming for this announcement: Two jet airplanes have been flown directly into the twin towers of the World Trade Center in New York City. Both towers were extensively damaged. Repeating, two jet airplanes have been flown directly into the World Trade Center towers in New York City. Hundreds or thousands of casualties are expected."

Jack, like the rest of the country, was stunned and uncomprehending. One plane could have been an accident, but two? Rather than continue on to the ailing oil rig, he threw the truck into an immediate U-turn, kicking up a huge plume of dust on the rutted dirt road. Minutes later he sped up to his parents' house and jumped from the cab, not even taking time to shut the truck off.

The television was on in the house, as he expected it would be. His mother was using her apron to dab at her eyes while his father stood, fists clenched at his sides. "I'll be goddamned," he repeated as the images of the planes crashing into the towers was shown over and over. Every time Jack tried to ask his father a question, his father shushed him and turned the television up a little louder. Every channel carried the same image, in addition to the announcement that another plane had crashed into the Pentagon building, and a short time later, a fourth went down in the Pennsylvania countryside, no doubt killing all aboard. Jack and his family watched the towers fall again and again while news crews scrambled to piece the story together. There was no doubt it was an act of terrorism, however, brought right to the American people.

By midafternoon most viewers had seen enough; the evening news would probably have a comprehensive update, they reasoned, and began to drift back to their lives, their jobs. Jack reluctantly did the same, heading back out to rig nine. When he arrived, the crew was somber. There was no need to ask if everyone had seen the news. Jack went to work on replacing a section of pipe, but as he worked he became angrier and angrier. How dare they — whoever they were? By the time he was finished he was ready to pick up one of the heavy wrenches and just beat something, and he could tell a few of the other guys felt the same way. The men with families just wanted to go home, but Jack and a few of the other single guys headed to Sally's Bar and Grill, in unspoken agreement to get drunk and raise some hell. A six-pack each later, their refrain had become, "We should go kick their asses." Jack awoke the next morning in the bed of his pickup, parked in front of the Marine Corps recruiting office, and he wasn't alone in waiting for it to open.

Chapter Two

In Las Vegas Bruce Barnes watched the coverage of the planes flying into the towers but unlike Jack, he had no motivation to enlist, donate, or otherwise become involved. He had quite enough on his plate taking a few classes at the community college and working as an orderly in a busy emergency department. Even though he had worked for several years in such a capacity, one tragedy still surprised him—the number of men, women, and even children who are abandoned, or simply unclaimed, in emergency rooms every year. There were families who simply didn't want to deal with grandpa's Alzheimer's during the holidays or who wouldn't identify a teenage driver in an accident where others were killed for fear of being drawn into a legal tangle themselves. There were others who were the simple victims of neglect and abuse and were simply swept into the system.

Barnes was more upset about these abandoned souls than he was about the countless victims of violence and ravaging illnesses that he saw wheeled into the hospital every day. He didn't need a psychiatrist to explain it to him, either. After being put up for adoption at the advanced age of four (he *knew* his mother, for God's sake!), he had suffered through a series of foster homes, some worse than others, with the certain knowledge that his own mother hadn't wanted him, nor would anyone else. He did his best to essentially disappear, or to not exist, and he was aided in this by his appearance. His hair was neither brown nor blonde, he wasn't big as a boy, but not small either. He was soft-spoken and few could ever remember hearing him laugh, or swear, for that matter. He wore what clothes were given him, seemingly indifferent to what impression he made on others. Bruce had few friends, but neither did he have enemies.

The hospital orderly job was perfect for him. There were always dozens of orderlies on duty and the doctors and nurses barked orders at them as if they were interchangeable, which, of course, they were. Some of them, especially the younger women, it seemed, sought to be recognized by the doctors and when things were slow in the emergency department the women went out of their way to be conspicuous. Bruce saw the flirtations for what they were.

"Hey, you, get bay five cleaned up and tell triage we can take another patient in five minutes," one of the residents yelled at Bruce, who didn't even bother to reply, just pulled on another set of gloves and headed to bay five where the treatment of a gunshot victim had left the floor littered with bloody ABD pads, soiled gloves and linen, torn packages of gauze and pools of fluids. Bruce worked almost mechanically, collecting the detritus, disposing of it according to hospital protocol, then giving the treatment bay one last inspection to see that everything was where it should be.

The one true talent Bruce possessed was his ability to see patterns and relationships quite clearly. He wasn't to the point of being obsessive-compulsive about it, but did give his mind a chance to exercise, as it were, while he carried out the most mundane tasks. One of the patterns he saw quite clearly was that the number of abandoned patients grew exponentially around the holidays or even around major sporting events such as the Superbowl.

The night before Thanksgiving, Bruce's theory was confirmed once again when a ward clerk coming on shift noticed an elderly man in a wheelchair outside the entrance to the emergency department. He was well-groomed with a thick head of silver hair, clean blue pajamas and a dark blue velvet robe with matching slippers. He sat serenely, humming to himself, in the 40-degree temperature made even colder by wind sweeping down from the mountains to the desert floor. When the triage staff asked him if perhaps a family member would be along shortly after parking the car, he continued to hum, not responding to any questions.

"Looks like we got another one," the harried triage nurse complained. "Get him into bay one and see if Dr. Christensen can take a look at him." Bruce stood by as another orderly wheeled the elderly gentleman away from triage.

"So, what happens to him if there's nothing wrong physically?" Bruce asked. "Do they just admit him for a few days until the family returns?"

"Hell no, we're not going to admit him," the triage nurse responded incredulously. "That's a thousand dollars a day, and no way the hospital is eating that." She slapped a 'Patient Name Unknown' label on the sign-in sheet and turned to her computer to log in the scanty details about his arrival. "They'll probably pack him up and ship him out to The Grove as soon as Christensen clears him."

Bruce persisted. "The Grove?"

The triage nurse deigned to talk to him, seeing no other patients in the waiting room. "The Grove is a nursing home out in Pahrump. There's a lot of them out there that take these kinds of patients."

Bruce laughed despite himself. "There isn't likely to be a 'grove' of anything in Pahrump unless it's tumbleweeds."

"It could be called the Taj Mahal for all I care," she said. "That's where they'll stick him, problem solved. Now go back to work."

Bruce slouched away from her desk, but during the next few hours of his shift he found excuses to stop by bay one and see if the man's situation had changed. It had not. He continued to smile benevolently and hum the same tune over and over. The doctor had given him a cursory examination and called for the transport team. The Grove would be alerted about a new arrival.

Just as he was about to clock out, Bruce heard Dr. Christensen complain to one of the nurses. "Damn transporters say it's too late to drive out to Pahrump. We're supposed to sit on him until they're good and ready." Bruce didn't hear the nurse's reply but knew she would be agreeing with the doctor's assessment no matter what.

"Uh, sir," Bruce began, trying to get the doctor's attention. "Sir?" The doctor looked up from charting on the computer, so Bruce plunged ahead. "I live near Pahrump and I could take him now, you know, on my way home."

The doctor shook his head and the nurse laughed. "Yeah, that's just what we need, just let the employees take patients home with them. That would solve the over-crowding." The two continued to laugh and Bruce stood there red-faced, but it bothered him a lot, not his own humiliation, but the plight of the gentleman who was someone's father, husband, brother, whatever. After he slid his identification badge through the time-keeping system, he made up his mind, quickly walking back to bay one and maneuvering the man's wheelchair into the hall, announcing to no one in particular, "We'll get this room available in just a minute." He wheeled the man back out to triage and out to the circular driveway the transport team always used, carefully setting the brakes on the wheelchair. Then he sprinted across the parking lot to his own car.

Chapter Three

Bruce pulled his car under the canopied entryway, thankful for the first time that he drove a big, older Chevy Impala. He left the motor idling and ducked around to open the passenger side door. To his surprise, the gentleman stood up uncertainly and, holding onto the door for support, eased himself into the car. Bruce shut the door and maneuvered the wheelchair into the back seat. Up to this moment he hadn't even considered the enormity of what he was doing, but damn it, it was just wrong to throw someone away!

He pulled quickly away from the hospital and headed for Blue Diamond Road, leading him west out of Las Vegas. Bruce had no intention of dumping the old man at The Grove, even if he had known how to find it, and instead headed for his apartment complex at the edge of town, near the turnoff to Red Rock Canyon. When he came to town nearly a year ago the complex was offering a promotion on two-bedroom units, so Bruce signed the lease, thinking perhaps it would be nice to have a roommate. That never happened but Bruce furnished the guest room anyway, although no one had ever visited.

Bruce watched the elderly man. He appeared not to be watching the scenery or anything else. He just continued to hum and stare straight ahead, the same benign smile in place. When Bruce finally pulled into his assigned carport space, the man made no move to undo his seatbelt, but didn't resist when Bruce reached across him to do so. He wrestled the wheelchair out of the back seat, then opened the passenger door. Once again, the man maneuvered into the chair on his own and allowed himself to be pushed along the sidewalk to Bruce's front door. Bruce nearly lost him in the shrubbery, having forgotten to set the brakes on the chair while he fumbled for his keys, but the lurching of the chair did nothing to change the man's calm demeanor.

Bruce knew every trick for maneuvering a wheelchair, but the narrow hallways of his apartment would present a challenge. Up to this point, Bruce hadn't said a word to his new charge. "Are you hungry?" he attempted, getting no response. "Do you need to use the bathroom?" He must, Bruce thought, as it had been hours since he was first brought into the emergency department. Was he even continent? Bruce had dealt with that issue countless times at work but hoped it wouldn't be one tonight. He wheeled the chair to the door of the single bathroom, and again the man surprised him by standing and walking unassisted to the toilet. Bruce left the chair in place but backed off to give him some privacy until he heard the toilet flush.

"Well, great, that's great," Bruce said with enthusiasm. "Now, how about something to eat?" Bruce had basically two specialties, a grilled cheese sandwich or scrambled eggs. The loaf of bread looked like it was well on its way to becoming a science experiment, but he did have a dozen eggs and some cheese and set about fixing them both something to eat. He had finally adjusted to working the night shift and was usually able to stay up for a few hours when he got home, watching the late-night talk shows, sometimes having a beer or two. Tonight, he had too many thoughts ricocheting around in his head to think about a beer or the television.

As he put the plate down in front of the man, he suddenly realized something else. "Well, I'm going to have to call you something, aren't I, if you can't tell me your name." He studied the man's patrician face and thick silver hair. "Something like Bob or Bill is too plain, I think." Bruce tried to recall the name of a movie star that frequently played the role of a friendly family physician but came up blank. "I think maybe Philip would be good, unless you object?" The man said nothing but he did pick up his fork to eat, another good sign as far as Bruce was concerned.

Chapter Four

As the adrenaline wore off and the consequences of Bruce's decision started to dawn on him, he found he was simply exhausted and he figured the old man must be as well. "Okay, bedtime for the boys," he called out cheerfully from the kitchen. It was close to four in the morning and Bruce's usual bedtime; he normally slept until noon, then spent the afternoon puttering around the apartment or out by the complex's swimming pool. The complex had lots of amenities, but as far as Bruce had seen, no one ever came out of their apartments to use any of them. He had yet to meet, or even see, his neighbors.

Bruce turned down the bed in the spare room and closed the black-out drapes, a necessity for a day-sleeper living in the desert. He brought his new roommate in, helped him stand and got him out of his robe, maneuvering him onto the side of the bed so he also get his slippers off. 'Philip' didn't resist and swung his own legs up onto the mattress, appearing to settle back comfortably into the pillows. Bruce parked the wheelchair next to the bed and wondered if he should leave a light on or just what would make his guest most comfortable.

As he went to hang the robe on a hook at the back of the bedroom door, he heard a slight tinkling sound from one of the pockets. "Oh, fine, did they leave you fifty cents so you could call for a ride home?" he muttered under his breath. He was very surprised to pull out a nubby silver chain threaded through a classic military dog tag. The dog tag was worn nearly smooth by years of handling, but the pertinent details were still readable. Bruce sat in the wheelchair. "So, you're Carl Nielsen, type O blood, born in 1909, so that makes you, what? 92? Wow, you look good for 92." Bruce extended his hand to the man, "I'm Bruce Barnes, pleased to meet you Carl Nielsen." Carl simply continued to hum and didn't raise his hand.

Bruce sat there fingering the dog tags and thought, "Well, now we know who you are and we can find your family and…yeah, the people who abandoned you in an unfamiliar ER." After a while, he could feel his eyes closing and so shut the light off in Carl's room, as he had already come to think of it, and moved off to his own bedroom. He left Carl's door open a notch and a small light on in the kitchen. He stripped down to his boxers and was asleep by the time his head hit the pillow.

But Bruce wasn't asleep for long before being awakened by a guttural growl that grew into a scream. He at first thought it was a nightmare, which it was, but not his. He raced into Carl's room and found the old man sitting bolt upright, clutching the sheet in front of him, screaming, eyes clamped shut. It was seven o'clock in the morning but the black-out drapes made it seem like midnight. "Hey, Carl, easy, easy," he said, draping his arm around the man's shoulders and trying to ease him back down in bed. Carl stopped screaming but remained as stiff as a board, his fingers white as the sheet they continued to clutch. Finally, after about ten minutes, he relaxed and resumed humming in his tuneless way. Bruce tucked him back under the covers, this time putting Carl's dog tags in his hand. He left both bedroom doors open but knew sleep would be impossible.

Finally, Bruce dressed in a pair of sweats and a t-shirt and picked up the phone. He couldn't leave the old man alone just yet and would have to call in sick, the first time he had ever done so. Truly, his jangled nerves from the long evening had made him about half-sick, he rationalized. The charge nurse in the ER accepted his excuse about a 'fast-moving stomach bug' and told him to stay home until he was sure he wasn't contagious. He looked in on Carl who appeared to be sleeping, then plopped down on the couch, hoping to at least get a nap.

His alarm went off at two p.m., an hour before his shift would have started, and he awakened on the couch startled to find Carl sitting in his wheelchair in front of the television, although he hadn't turned it on. "Good morning, or I should say, good afternoon," Bruce began, again getting no response. "I need a shower, and you probably do, too," he said mostly to himself. "And then something to eat, how about that?" Carl half-smiled but said nothing.

Bruce was happy he had bought extra bath towels when he furnished the guest room, so he grabbed one and wheeled Carl to the shower. He once again took off the man's robe and mimicked taking off his pajamas. Carl watched him but made no move to do anything until Bruce turned the shower on, at which point he pulled the pajama top over his head and hefted himself slightly in the wheelchair to remove the bottom. Bruce helped him to stand and he walked into the shower without further assistance, putting his hand out until Bruce filled it with shampoo. He once again let the man have his privacy although left the bathroom door open. He'd have to think about getting Carl a change of clothing, he realized, Carl being much taller and thinner than Bruce. And he had to go grocery shopping; a dozen eggs would only last so long.

Chapter Five

While other men wondered how long they would last in boot camp, for Jack and the other West Texas boys, it was a breeze, as accustomed as they were to being out in the elements and doing hard physical work. Seeing his lack of a high school diploma, Jack was assigned to an infantry squadron, which suited him just fine. He simply wanted to go kill people. The constant yelling, threatening, demeaning behavior of the drill sergeants did nothing to diminish the desire he felt on seeing the towers topple; if anything, the stress motivated him even more. He was especially careful to hide any of his mechanical aptitude, fearing he would be stuck out of the action in some rear echelon, repairing tanks or whatever. Being a dumb 'grunt' would suit him just fine.

Jack felt they would be likely deployed to some ground unit in Afghanistan, and he relished the excitement of house-to-house searches and hand-to-hand combat, some of which he and the others in his unit experienced on a simulated basis during training. He was surprised, therefore, to learn that they would be shipping out to Norfolk, Virginia, there to join a FAST unit (Fleet Anti-Terrorism Security Force) on a Navy destroyer escorting the carrier, USS *Theodore Roosevelt*, all part of a carrier strike group. Jack had never been on a boat bigger than a 16-foot ski boat, and although he would rather have deployed immediately into combat, he looked forward to the experience nonetheless.

Less than a week later, he had changed his mind. The days were tediously long, spent in drills that seemed to have little purpose, moving weapons from one location to the other and then back again, spending countless monotonous hours cleaning weapons and equally monotonous hours in target practice on floating targets. The Navy personnel had their own drills although they did interact with the Marines on basic fire protection drills or man-overboard scenarios. Jack and the others spent hours discussing what life must be like on the giant carrier; the decks always looked like a hive of activity with jets taking off and landing, equipment being moved up and down giant elevators, and an endless barrage of announcements blaring over the loud speakers. They were particularly fascinated by how the big ship was fueled by other ships also in the escort party. But the pace was too slow to suit Jack. They seemed to progress in an almost stately fashion, and although their ultimate destination had not been announced, most assumed it would be the Persian Gulf.

In the evenings the crew played cards, told stories, cleaned weapons, and did whatever it took to pass the time, although there were drills, often unannounced, at night as well. Jack found that he had an uncanny ability to play 21 and soon exhausted the number of Marines who would put up a few bucks to play with him. He was dealt an ace and would draw the jack of spades so often that he soon had a new nickname, Black Jack Hamilton. When a few of the cards were blown away from a deck, he managed to snag the jack of spades and tucked it in his helmet, his new emblem, although his sergeant told him it just made for a sharper target on his head.

So, weeks went by and at last they did steam into the Persian Gulf to be part of Operation Enduring Freedom in which they would go after al-Qaeda, the Islamist group having claimed responsibility for the 9/11 attacks. The amount of drills increased and Jack watched the carrier, timing jets within seconds of each other being shot off the deck like cannons and snared by the hook as they landed, instantly swarmed by mechanics and re-fueling personnel. He knew he could have been part of that elite group but convinced himself that once he was in combat he'd forget all about the carrier.

But his wish came sooner than he expected. During a lull between drills, several of the Marines and a few Navy personnel stood looking out over the seas when suddenly the destroyer shuddered and lurched violently, throwing at least a dozen of them overboard, Jack included, along with a shower of flaming shrapnel created from a hole blown in the side of the destroyer. The general quarters alarm sounded immediately, directing everyone to preassigned stations due to an imminent threat. As stunned as Jack was he couldn't help thinking that the threat should have been imminent five minutes before it happened, not thirty seconds afterwards.

The Gulf waters were choppy from the wave action created by the carrier and all of its escort ships, in addition to a light wind, so it was difficult for Jack to see exactly how many men had been thrown violently into the sea, but he spotted at least a dozen; only some of them looked to still be alive. He jettisoned his heavy steel-toed boots and as much gear as possible, then began to swim toward the closest soldier, acutely aware of how much his uniform weighed him down.

The claxon continued to sound general quarters on all the ships in the convoy, but over all of that he heard the sound of helicopters, too. The first chopper he could see clearly appeared to have a news cameraman hanging partway out the door; Jack felt like flipping him off but continued to swim. The military's new policy of allowing "embedded" news crews seemed like an especially foolish idea about now, Jack thought as he continued to swim.

He reached the first Marine and it was clear he was already dead, probably from the shock of the concussion when the destroyer was hit, but Jack held onto him and looked up to see another helicopter lowering a line and with a hook attached. He hooked the dead man up through his belt loops and motioned for the bird to take him up. Another line dropped seconds later and Jack paddled to a Navy man, barely conscious but able to slip his arms through the dropped line and be pulled up to the chopper. The film crew continued to hover overhead, the downwash from the rotor blades obscuring Jack's vision even further. His arms were aching from the effort of fighting the waves and keeping his head above water to spot more men; he had no idea how long he was in the water until he finally saw no other men.

The next thing Jack felt, however, was the whizz of machine gun bullets hitting the water all around him. "WTF!! Now they're shooting at me!" Jack was incredulous until he saw the intended targets—a swarm of sharks attracted by the blood in the water. This time when the line was dropped, Jack took it eagerly and ascended out of reach, the film crew having captured the entire rescue effort for the six o'clock news.

Chapter Six

The image of Jack clinging to the line with one arm, the other raised in a thumbs-up salute, T-shirt in tatters, but with him flashing a dazzling smile went round the world. When he was finally hoisted into the chopper, the crew on board enthusiastically slapped him on the back but wanted to strap him to a stretcher. "No way, dude, I'm fine," Jack protested, adrenalin still pounding through his system. "I'm walkin' off this bird." He enjoyed his aerial view for a few more seconds until the helicopter began its descent to the carrier deck, the wounded destroyer having been mostly evacuated by now.

Sailors and Marines on board the carrier rushed to shake Jack's hand or hug him roughly but when the celebration died down, Jack snapped to attention, acknowledging the approach of the carrier strike group's admiral. The other Marines and Navy men followed suit and even though the planes and helicopters still took off and landed at a furious pace, that section of the deck took on an almost formal air. "At ease, men," the admiral announced, striding forward to firmly shake Jack's hand. "Excellent job out there, sergeant!"

"Thank you, sir. We're trained, sir, no man left behind, sir."

"So you are, so you are, son." With that, the commander dismissed the men, including Jack. "Back to duty!"

Back in Washington, D.C., the rescue had been scrutinized quite closely. "I'm telling you—this country needs a hero and that's our boy right damn there!" The Senator reviewed the news coverage with the President and his advisors.

"I don't know," one of the advisors said hesitantly. "Is he Mexican?"

"Oh for chrissakes, he's not Mexican," the Senator snapped back, "and if he was, it would be that much better to pick up the Hispanic vote!"

The President had stayed out of the debate but finally interjected. "So, what do you propose? Do we bring him here for a medal ceremony? Should I maybe go there and give all the troops a boost while we give him the medal?"

The advisors, almost in unison, responded. "Go there? Not a chance at this point." The military men in the room murmured their concurrence, pointing out that it still wasn't clear who had bombed the destroyer, no one group stepping forward to take credit as of yet. The discussion went round and round for another few minutes, until the Senator finally stood.

"I propose we bring him here, immediately, fly him off that carrier tonight, and set up a ceremony in the Rose Garden for Tuesday." He paused. "But that can't be the end of it. We need to *use* this kid and *use* him hard."

The President and his advisors looked quizzically at the senior Senator. "We need to have him speaking at every town hall meeting, every recruiting center—hell, maybe even the United Nations." He leaned forward onto the President's desk for emphasis. "We need to show the world that this is what America is about—that we don't take crap from anyone, we don't leave our men whistling in the wind, and we know what it takes to get the job done and keep this country safe. Period!"

One of the advisors known for his cynical view of virtually every opportunity said quietly, "Do we know if this kid can even string two words together?"

Another press advisor snapped, "That doesn't matter, Howard. We'll be writing his damn speeches!"

To which Howard responded, "Do we know if he can even read them? Some of the enlisted…"

The President finally tired of the whole debate. "It's settled. Get him off the carrier, set up the Rose Garden ceremony, find out what medal he ought to get." He pointed at the press advisor. "And find out everything you can about him—especially if he can read." He sighed and left the room. The media spin would crank into high gear.

Word went out immediately to the carrier, and Jack was subsequently called to the bridge where the admiral and several other officers waited. He saluted immediately but was told to stand at ease. The admiral sat in one of the swivel chairs and motioned for the others to do the same, although Jack remained standing. "It appears we're going to be sending you stateside in a few hours," he began. He expected Jack to look pleased but instead saw the young soldier immediately become frustrated.

"Permission to speak freely, sir?" When the admiral nodded, Jack continued. "I wasn't injured at all, fit as a fiddle the medics said."

"No, Jack, it has nothing to do with your readiness," the admiral explained. "It seems they want to give you a medal and make an example of you—a source of pride for the whole country."

"Begging your pardon sir, with all due respect, I just want to see some combat, sir, make my country proud that way."

The admiral and the others laughed heartily. "That wasn't enough combat for you!" Jack flushed deeply but said nothing for the moment. After the officers stopped laughing, the admiral continued seriously. "What you did yesterday was an act of bravery and everyone in the country respects that. It's important for all of them to see the quality and caliber of men we have serving, so consider it an honor and do your best to continue to make us proud."

Jack stiffened his shoulders a bit more to hide his disappointment. "Thank you, sir. I will, sir."

"That's all then. Be ready to lift off at 1600. Dismissed."

Jack wound his way back down to his bunk, his frustration finally getting the best of him as he slammed his fist into the bulkhead. As he jammed his gear into a duffle, one of the other sailors asked what Jack was doing. "Oh, they're sending me to Washington so the President can give me a goddamn medal," he snarled.

The other men stopped what they were doing to look at him in amazement until one said what they were all thinking, "You're pissed that you're getting out of here and getting a medal. Shit, boy, maybe you got salt water in your ears yesterday." Jack continued packing and the other sailors drifted away shaking their heads.

Up on the bridge, the admiral was shaking his, too. "Combat, he thought, that boy'll probably see plenty of combat when he starts dealing with those Washington types."

Chapter Seven

Bruce was dealing with his own version of the war, but this was World War II. Carl's night terrors, if that's what they were, persisted and it didn't take long to wear Bruce to a frazzle. He'd read about PTSD in soldiers and had seen dozens of them brought into the emergency department over the years suffering from hallucinations, suicidal rages and suicide attempts. After two days of calling in sick, however, Bruce had to return to work, which meant he had to leave Carl alone for as long as 10 hours.

"Okay, I have to go to work," Bruce told Carl across the breakfast table. He really didn't know how much Carl listened or understood, but he continued. "So, I'm leaving two sandwiches in the refrigerator, there's fruit here on the counter and bottled water." Carl stared placidly as Bruce wheeled him in front of the television set. What to put on for the old soldier? CNN was too repetitive, Fox too right-wing, the cartoon channel too insulting if Carl still had his wits about him. Bruce finally settled on a station that ran mostly classic movies. He placed the remote in Carl's hand but expected to find it untouched when he returned near midnight. As he left the apartment he hesitated. Normally he would lock the regular lock and the deadbolt, but what if something happened and Carl was locked in? Reluctantly, he pushed the button in the regular lock and headed for his car.

Fortunately, there wasn't a full moon, a big sporting event or rock concert in Las Vegas that night so the ER was relatively quiet. Bruce decided to use the time to make some discrete inquiries, starting with the crusty triage nurse. "You know that old guy the other night, the one with the gray hair that was brought in about ten? You sent him back to Dr. Christensen?"

"Oh, gee, let me think. When have I ever seen an old guy come into the ER?" she replied sarcastically.

"Oh come on, you know the one that was all by himself, no identification or anything? You said he'd be going to The Grove in Pahrump?"

"Vaguely. Really kiddo, I can't be bothered trying to remember every patient through the door," the nurse told Bruce dismissively. "Don't you have a room to prep?"

Bruce left the desk and returned to the department where he found Dr. Christensen once again on call, but this time just playing solitaire on one of the computer screens. "Good evening, sir," Bruce began. Dr. Christensen looked his way and yawned.

"What's up, dude?"

"Oh, nothing, I mean, well," Bruce stammered. "Do you remember a couple nights ago you examined an old man who had just been dumped in his wheelchair in the driveway outside the department? He didn't talk at all, just sort of hummed."

"Oh, yeah, and you were the one who volunteered to take him out to Pahrump! I certainly remember that," he laughed. "What about him?"

"Well, what happens to people like that if no one, uh, claims them?"

"Usually whatever facility they end up in does the legal work to obtain custodial care and then they just take care of them and bill the State, I guess." The doctor thought for a minute. "It doesn't seem right, but I guess the alternative could be much worse in terms of abuse or neglect." He turned back to the computer just as the announcement came through the department that a GSW was en route with an ETA of three minutes.

The next hour was a flurry of activity as the staff worked to stabilize the gunshot victim and dealt with two more ambulances filled with car crash survivors and a man purportedly poisoned by his wife. Bruce was amazed to see it was just minutes before the end of his shift when he finally took a minute to look at his watch. He was exhausted and sleep-deprived and longed to go home, but he was also concerned about what he would find. On the drive home he rolled down the windows and let the cool desert air revive him, all the while thinking about Dr. Christensen's comments about custodial care. Should he pursue that with Carl or simply deliver him to a care home, the original plan? He'd decide when he got back to the apartment.

Chapter Eight

He shouldn't have been surprised. Carl was pretty much as he'd left him, the television tuned to the same channel, the sandwiches uneaten, although Carl had drank some of the water and evidently used the bathroom as well. While Bruce threw the dried-out sandwich in the garbage, Carl continued his humming, rubbing his dog tags all the while. Bruce shut the television off and brought Carl to the table, putting the second sandwich in front of him. Carl placidly ate it but offered no comment. Bruce helped him through the same bathroom/bedroom routine as the previous two nights, then stretched out on the couch himself waiting for the screaming to begin.

He didn't have to wait long. Bruce had discovered that putting a light on and waking him up brought a stop to it, but the humming resumed immediately, often with greater intensity. Bruce felt it was some kind of coping mechanism for the old man, and even though he didn't look sick, he clearly was. But, he couldn't keep him awake 24/7 as a way to stave off the nightmares. The pattern continued for several days until Bruce finally had the insight to put a night light in Carl's room and also to have music playing lightly in the background. On nights when that failed, a shot of brandy seemed to do the trick and both men slept through the night.

Even though Carl never spoke, Bruce found he enjoyed the man's company nevertheless. He started looking for attorneys who handled adult custody matters and found one with offices a block from the courthouse downtown. He bought Carl a new pair of khakis and a blue polo shirt, inexpensive tennis shoes and a few pairs of socks and underwear. He looked like every other retiree on the streets of Las Vegas as Bruce loaded him into the car for the appointment with the attorney, a Mr. Joseph Sheridan.

When Bruce called for the appointment a secretary asked him for most of the pertinent details, so Sheridan had a file on the desk in front of him when Bruce and Carl were shown back to his office. Bruce had left out the salient detail of how he had "poached" Carl from placement in a nursing home, substituting the story that Carl was a very distant relative for whom no one in the family wished to take responsibility.

Sheridan stood when they entered and Bruce was surprised to see that he wore a high-quality suit with gold cufflinks and shoes buffed to a gleam. Given the relatively low price of $300 the secretary had quoted Bruce, he didn't expect half as much. "Welcome, I'm Joseph Sheridan," the attorney said, extending his hand to Carl who ignored it, then to Bruce, "make yourselves comfortable." He signaled the secretary to bring in some bottled waters and motioned both men to comfortable leather chairs in front of his desk.

"So, I understand you're seeking custodial care of Mr. Nielsen here..."

"Yes, nobody wants him," Bruce started. "I mean, that sounds terrible, but his family, I mean, our family, just can't take care of him." The attorney looked as placid as Carl, so Bruce continued. "I work in the healthcare field so I recognize the needs he has and I can provide the care for him." Carl chose that moment to start humming. "He hums, I think, to keep his PTSD in check, but you get used to it, at least I have." He realized it sounded like he was begging for the attorney's help, so he forced himself to stop talking.

"Let me explain how the process works, Mr. Barnes. I will file a petition with the court asking to grant you sole care and custody of Mr. Nielsen. That *is* what you want?" Bruce nodded enthusiastically. "Then, if no one from the family—your family—protests, the court will award you that responsibility."

Bruce had a dozen questions but asked simply, "And how long a process is that?"

Sheridan explained it might take a month or less. "Let me stress, though, it is a responsibility. You will be responsible for his total care. For instance, if he requires medical treatment in the hospital, you will be financially responsible, and by the same token, in the event of his demise, you will be his sole beneficiary of any estate that is found to exist." That hadn't even occurred to Bruce, and the attorney saw it readily in Bruce's surprised expression. "Have you made any inquiries as to the extent of his assets?"

"No, I, uh, I just assumed he didn't have any," Bruce said truthfully. "I mean he was just..." He couldn't continue with the actual explanation of how he found Carl, of course. "He's just an old man who needs some help."

The attorney studied Bruce for a moment. "Well, we have his social security number and date of birth, so we can make some inquiries about any government benefits that may be due him," he began, "and search for any bank accounts. That may take a few weeks as well." When Bruce didn't reply, Sheridan continued. "Do you want us to do that as well as file the petition?"

"If it wouldn't cost a lot more money, I guess you could," Bruce said slowly. "I work full-time on a three to eleven shift so it doesn't leave me much time to go calling on banks and all that." Then he realized he might have made a small mistake. "But, Carl is fine during the time I'm gone. He has food and he seems to enjoy the movie channels. He takes care of himself pretty well except for the not talking thing." Bruce realized he was rambling again.

"All right, Mr. Barnes, we'll get things started and I'll have my secretary let you know when the court hearing is set. You and Mr. Nielsen will both need to be in attendance." He stood and attempted once again to shake hands with Carl but settled for a hasty swipe of Bruce's hand. He escorted the duo to the hallway and Bruce stopped on the way out to write a check to the secretary.

Normally when he and Carl were in the car, Bruce tried to keep up a running one-sided conversation, pointing out anything he thought might be interesting, but today they drove home in silence. It hadn't even occurred to Bruce that Carl might have an estate. Wouldn't that be something?

Chapter Nine

Bruce took Carl shopping for slacks and a sports coat plus a tie in anticipation of the upcoming court date. Carl was his usual placidly cooperative self until the sales clerk began to measure his in-seam. Carl's eyes seemed to bug out of his head and he turned to Bruce, reaching out to him for the first time ever. Bruce, on the other hand, was nearly convulsed with laughter and the young salesman was simply mortified. They finally agreed on a rough estimate and Bruce escorted Carl into a dressing room; the slacks fit fine.

Sheridan's secretary called two weeks later giving Bruce the date and time of their court appearance and telling them which courtroom would be handling their case. She reassured him that Sheridan would meet with them in the hallway just a few minutes beforehand. She assured Bruce that despite their efforts, no other family members had come forward and the proceeding should be no more than a formality. The ensuing two weeks were much like every week beforehand. Carl still hadn't spoken but the night terrors were less frequent and he often ate the lunch Bruce left for him. Bruce thought the television channel might even have been changed occasionally. Carl still hummed.

When they arrived at the courthouse a half-hour early, Bruce saw Sheridan exiting another courtroom, a slim leather briefcase under one arm while he steered a young woman by the elbow. He nodded briefly to Bruce and took the woman off to a quieter corner for a brief conversation which seemed to resolve things for the woman who finally smiled at Sheridan and left the corridor.

"Gentlemen, how are you?" the lawyer asked, patting Carl on the shoulder and pumping Bruce's hand. "We're just over here in courtroom four. The judge handles a lot of these hearings, so there shouldn't be any surprises." He could detect Bruce's nervousness. "Just answer his questions, you know, keep it simple, and we'll be out of here in ten."

"Yes, sir, I'm just…I've never been in a courtroom before except on TV." He flushed. "Well, I've never been on TV either, but you know." He and Sheridan both had a laugh and made their way into the small courtroom, fitted out more like a boardroom, absent the jury box and the high dais many judges prefer. A bailiff was on hand to announce the judge's arrival. Bruce was surprised to see that he was young, perhaps only forty, although he wore tortoise-shell rimmed glasses giving him an owl-like appearance, and his robe was open enough to show a tweedy-looking sweater and bow tie.

Two cases preceded theirs, both dealing with the custody of minors. Social workers and attorneys handled the proceedings without the presence of parents or the children involved, another surprise to Bruce. Sheridan paid no attention but rose smoothly to attention when the Barnes/Nielsen case was called by the judge, introducing himself, Bruce and Carl formally, then quipping, "So, your honor, I hear you took a beating out at the Seven Hills tourney?"

The judge muttered something away from the microphone but was smiling when he finished, turning to Bruce. "So, I hope you know the responsibility you're taking on here for your...what is he?"

Before Bruce could say anything, Sheridan responded. "Mr. Nielsen is a distant relation to the petitioner. No other family member has stepped forward to provide care, temporarily or permanently, as Mr. Barnes has, your honor."

"All right, seeing no objections to the petition, full custody is awarded to Mr. Bruce Barnes." With that, the judge tapped his gavel lightly. "Good luck, Mr. Barnes. This is a good thing you're doing. Just try and keep it in perspective." Bruce nodded. "Dismissed."

Sheridan stuffed the Barnes/Nielsen folder back into his briefcase and motioned Bruce and Carl to follow him back out into the corridor.

"Well, you were right, that was pretty smooth," Bruce began.

"Yes, well now the rest of it needs to be handled," Sheridan interrupted him. He looked at his watch and said, "Look, why don't you come back to my office in about, say, 45 minutes. Get some lunch or something in the meantime. We've got a few things to go over." The lawyer rushed off, leaving Bruce to wonder how things would go taking Carl out to lunch for the first time. He found a little coffee shop next to the courthouse that clearly was used to serving people in a hurry to make their court appointments. Bruce ordered sandwiches for both of them and iced tea. Carl dutifully ate his sandwich and sipped at the tea before pushing it away.

"So, Carl, there's at least something you don't like," Bruce tried to joke. "Note to self, no iced tea for Carl." He noticed that even with the hustle and bustle of the courtroom and the strange surroundings, Carl had hummed very little that morning. Maybe the activity had a calming effect. Bruce should see if he could take Carl to work with him!

Sheridan was sitting at his secretary's desk when they returned, suit coat off and sleeves rolled up. "The half-day Kathy takes off can seem like an eternity," he complained to Bruce. I know she has her 'system' of filing things, but it's a complete mystery to me. Whatever happened to simple alphabetical?" Finally he located what he'd been looking for and ushered the two back to his office. "Remember what I said about looking into his estate?" Bruce nodded. "Well, we're about halfway through that process, but we did discover one thing that's going to be very helpful for you." Bruce perked up and the lawyer continued. "Carl is a veteran, which of course, you knew from the dog tags, and he has a lot of unused benefits."

"Like disability, or what?"

"No, more along the lines of assistance. He's eligible to have a caretaker come in, to the tune of about twelve hundred a month, maybe take over while you're at work." Bruce brightened considerably at that idea. "The Veterans Administration is notoriously slow with these things, but I think we can put in an expedited request since you really have no alternatives and have to work, etcetera, etcetera." He paused, reading through Kathy's notes. "It looks like you could have someone as soon as the end of the month." That was only ten days away. "You'd have to find that person, of course, and work out the details, but there are probably plenty of people at the hospital where you work that would like to pick up a few extra bucks and help you out in the process."

Bruce immediately thought of some the ward clerks earning minimum wage, but then realized any one of them might reveal his secret about snatching Carl. He'd think of some other way, instead. Las Vegas was awash in people needing second, or even third, jobs.

Sheridan snapped Bruce out of his reverie. "We did find a bank account that hasn't been touched in quite a while, apparently with his pension checks being direct-deposited. You need to go to the bank with the court documents from today, which you'll have in about a week, and get your name put on the account as executor. Come by next week and Kathy can give you all that stuff." He stood to signal the end of their meeting, once again looking at his watch. Bruce was almost too stunned to catch the implication, but finally jumped to his feet and pumped Sheridan's hand vigorously.

"Thank you, thank you so much. Yes, I'll see Kathy next week." He took Carl by the elbow and maneuvered him to the waiting wheelchair, although he had begun to suspect the old man didn't really need the chair at all; it had just been a way to park him at the ER.

Chapter Ten

Bruce went to a hospital across town from where he worked but actually only two miles from where he lived and studied the employee announcement boards. As he anticipated, there were several postings for people seeking second jobs, and one in particular that hoped to find a 3 p.m. to 11 p.m. assignment, identical to Bruce's work shift. He copied the number and called from his cell phone before leaving the parking lot. The young woman who answered said she could meet him in the hospital cafeteria on her break in about 15 minutes. She told him to sit near the windows overlooking the atrium and that she would be wearing bright pink scrubs.

Bruce recognized the petite Filipina immediately and motioned her to his table. He already had coffee and pastries waiting. After dispensing with the introductions, she jumped right in. "I have been a caregiver all my life, for my family and for friends, and my people have always been pleased."

He noticed that she didn't say 'patients' or 'clients' which he thought was a good sign that she actually thought of them as people. She went on about supplying references and a background check, but he had already made up his mind, based mostly on her infectious smile and can-do attitude. "Lea, I think you would be ideal. I wonder if you could come by and meet Carl, just see what you're getting into, and then you could let me know."

She clapped her hands together like a child and impulsively hugged him. "Oh, I know I'll like Carl." She got the address and told him she'd be by tomorrow at 1 p.m., leaving him time to show her around and get himself ready for work.

She was right on time the next day, something Bruce appreciated, and on entering the apartment went directly to Carl and gave him a quick hug, something Bruce had never done. Carl seemed to smile a little more broadly, Bruce thought, and suspended his humming. "That's what he does, hum," Bruce explained. "I think it helps him deal with stress from PTSD—at least that's my theory." He had already told Lea that Carl never spoke. "He can do a lot for himself, but I just don't like leaving him alone so long."

"Well, Carl, you're not alone now," Lea beamed at the elderly man. "You hum and I'll sing, and the time will just fly by, you watch." Her enthusiasm seemed contagious not only to Bruce but to Carl who looked directly at her. Bruce went to change into his own scrubs and showed Lea a list of instructions and his contact phone number.

"You can make out a list of what you need from the grocery store," Bruce said before he left for work, "and I'll pick them up the next day, or if you need anything else."

"We'll be fine. You go to work." She winked, "Somebody has to pay me, you know."

The change in Carl even a week later was remarkable. He still didn't speak but he seemed almost happy, the night terrors had almost disappeared and when he hummed it seemed more like a real song. It had to be Lea's influence, Bruce realized, and thought perhaps if he was to be the one to spend eight hours with the cute young woman he'd be humming a tune too! One of the most interesting parts of Carl's transformation, however, was in his eating habits. With Bruce he had pretty much subsisted on cold sandwiches and occasional scrambled eggs, but Lea had begun making Filipino food, lumpia, adobo, pancit and vegetables that Bruce had never seen. Carl ate all of it, and heartily, at that. Bruce wondered if Carl had been stationed in the Philippines at one time, perhaps he even had a Filipino bride? Bruce doubted the latter after having seen how devoted Lea appeared to be to anyone she considered family. If Carl had married into a Filipino family he wouldn't have been parked outside an emergency department, Bruce was certain.

The arrangement worked beautifully. The three even celebrated Carl's birthday with a cake, although Lea ended up blowing out the candles for Carl. The occasion did remind Bruce that Carl was now 93, an advanced age by any standard. He had taken Carl for a check-up at a combination insta-care/family practice clinic and found the old man had hypertension, a heart murmur and a bruit over one carotid artery, but even the doctor said, "I should be doing that well at my age, much less 93."

But, sadly, everything wears out and Carl was no exception. Lea called Bruce at work early one evening in tears and before she said a word, Bruce knew. He hurriedly clocked out of work and drove home as fast as he dared. Lea was waiting for him on the front step, still crying. "I went into the kitchen just for a few minutes to get dinner ready, but when I came back…" and she broke down again. Bruce hugged her and went into the apartment. He had to fight back his own tears when he saw Carl slumped sideways on the couch. He checked for a pulse, knowing Lea would already have done the same; finding none, he called 9-1-1 and went back out to the porch to be with Lea and await the police and ambulance.

Days later Carl was laid to rest after a funeral in one of the local Filipino churches where Lea was a member. Bruce felt certain Carl would have enjoyed the singing and heartfelt prayers that Lea's family delivered. She confessed to Bruce that during his time at work she had often invited other members of her family over to 'visit' with Carl, something she said he seemed to enjoy.

Chapter Eleven

Bruce didn't imagine he would see Lea after the funeral, but he paid her as if she had worked the full month and told her he would always be her friend. She was still too overcome to do more than nod and hug him briefly before she left with her family. The apartment seemed doubly empty when he went home, and actually he was glad of the opportunity to go to work that night.

He went back to his usual routine for a few days, but finally 'things' just had to be dealt with. He boxed up Carl's meager wardrobe for a trip to Goodwill, although he kept his dog tags; he thought about wearing them himself, but that seemed wrong and instead settled them next to the only sports trophy he had ever won in high school—and that was only because every member of the team had received one.

The envelope that had been sitting on top of the refrigerator ever since their visit with the attorney, Sheridan, finally demanded Bruce's attention. "The Estate of Carl Nielsen" was printed in calligraphy (must be a hobby of his secretary, Bruce thought idly). The first several paragraphs simply established Carl's identity and the custodial disposition to Bruce. It also listed all attempts made to elicit any response from any other family members and ultimately declared Bruce the sole heir and beneficiary of Carl's estate, all pretty straightforward, as Sheridan said it would be.

On the second page things got more interesting. Under the heading 'Real Estate and Real Property' a one-word description sufficed: None.

Under the heading 'Securities, Annuities and Monetary Investments' was listed a figure of $173,800 as of close of business June 18, 2015. It identified two different brokerage firms. Bruce re-read the short listing three times but still couldn't comprehend it.

The last heading of 'Pensions and Other Payments Due' was an equally astounding figure of $218,300. Suddenly Bruce had more money than he ever anticipated having in his lifetime. A little part of him wished he knew where Carl's family was—not to share with them—to say, "See what you lost?" That impulse passed in a second and was replaced by an even sadder thought. If they knew he had these kinds of assets and still couldn't bring themselves to take care of him, what kind of people were they anyway?

He put the documents back in the envelope and replaced it on top of the refrigerator, then snatched it back. Maybe it should go in a safety deposit box? He didn't have one, but he could get one, he reasoned. But no, he'd need the legal paperwork to access the money, transfer it into his name. He looked at the clock and realized he had only twenty minutes to dress and race into work. Work? Should he still keep his job? He had read about lottery winners who thought they'd still work at their menial jobs. Wonder how long that lasted? He'd think about it more tonight. He wasn't the type of person to just walk off a job without giving notice, after all.

His shift went by in a blur. He had begun to think in terms of "BC" as Before Carl and "AC" After Carl. Whereas BC the menial tasks that came with being an orderly just seemed routine, now, AC, they were onerous and demeaning. It didn't take Bruce long to realize that he could not continue this kind of a job with that kind of money sitting in the bank. Nor could he see himself just blowing the money on a new Corvette or even buying a house in Vegas' bloated housing market. He somehow thought Carl would expect better of him.

Driving home down Maryland Parkway took him past the University of Nevada, a place he'd only visited to take in a basketball game. But tonight it took on a greater significance. He could go to college, be a serious full-time student and actually pursue a career. He resolved to go by the admissions office as soon as he awoke the next day. He went straight to bed when he got home and slept better than he could ever remember.

Bruce awoke refreshed and resolved. He re-read the legal documents over toast and coffee. By ten he was at the admissions office, picking up a course catalog and an application. An admissions counselor agreed to see him for a few minutes and told him what documentation he would need to accompany the application. Fall quarter enrollment would begin in a few short days. He went to a chain restaurant near the college, one frequented by students, and imagined himself part of this new group. He began to make a list of the things he needed to do, first being to transfer the money into his name. He would also look for an apartment close to campus.

His second epiphany in as many days came when he looked at the list of possible majors. He would major in health care administration with a minor in accounting to take advantage of his strengths in seeing patterns and having worked in healthcare for a few years already. Accounting, he thought, was a seemingly dull choice but as it would turn out, one with options for some creativity as well.

Chapter Twelve

The military establishment was going to be forced to be creative as well. The rescue had been televised almost as much as the 9/11 attacks, it seemed, and when it was announced that the brave Marine would be meeting with the President to accept the Medal of Honor, America expected to see that ceremony over and over, too.

Bruce was in the midst of registering for his classes on the Las Vegas campus on the morning of the ceremony and listened briefly to the CNN analyst. "This moment of heroism and glory has united the country like no other in recent memory," the commentator said solemnly. Another student who also stopped to listen said, "Yeah, that guy's the luckiest guy on earth." Bruce turned to him. "He's gonna get more women than he knows what to do with." The other student laughed and wandered off, leaving Bruce to silently agree with him and wonder if he, Bruce, could have been capable of the same bravery. You never know what you're capable of, he decided, and went back to selecting his classes.

The White House pulled out all the stops for the Rose Garden ceremony; even the weather cooperated with the cherry blossom trees lining the Potomac off in the background. Dignitaries from not only the military, but business and industry, especially those in Texas, and the government were slated to attend. Security at all public events had been tightened since the 9/11 attacks, and every guest, regardless of his or her status would have to pass through metal detectors and perhaps even be subject to a personal search by a member of the special White House police.

At about the same time Jack was leaving the carrier, FBI agents were arriving at his parents' home in Andrews, Texas, some thirty miles north of Midland. When the standard black Suburban rolled into the dusty driveway, Jack's father was looking out the window monitoring its approach. "Hon, we're fixin' to have company," he yelled to his wife out in the laundry room. "Looks like the FBI, just like on TV." When the men climbed out of the SUV, his opinion was confirmed. He straightened the collar on his shirt and moved to open the door and greet them on the porch.

"Ernest Hamilton?" the shorter of the two agents asked, pulling his credentials out of his pocket at the same time. The other agent hung back a few steps, not knowing what to expect in the way of a greeting.

"Yessir, welcome to my home today," the elder Hamilton replied, spreading his arms broadly and perhaps laying on the West Texas accent a little more heavily than usual. "Come on up here out of that heat and dust. Can't feel real good in those black suits!" He laughed and the agents had to chuckle as well.

"First off, sir, let me assure you no trouble has come to your son. He's just fine," the second agent said with a bit of a Texas accent himself. By this time

Jack's mother had come out onto the porch, smiling nervously.

"You say Jack's fine," she repeated. "Well, then what brings you here?" The agent started to answer, but she cut him off. "I'm so sorry, gentlemen. Let's have some iced tea, shall we?" She ducked back into the house before they could see her start to cry with relief.

When she returned with four cold glasses of tea, the agents accepted gratefully and the Texan began again. "Ma'am, sir, the President of the United States has sent us here today to meet you folks and tell you the big news about your fine boy." He took a sip of the tea, trying not to grimace at the sweetness. "Jack is to receive the Medal of Honor from the President himself this Tuesday in Washington, D.C., and naturally the President wants you both to be there for that proud moment." He had more or less finished his prepared speech and waited for their reactions.

"That's my book club day," Rose Hamilton said, looking thoughtful, "although I suppose Judy could take it over just that once."

Ernest looked equally thoughtful. "Well, I was supposed to speak at Kiwanis," hesitating, "but boy I hate making speeches." He looked at his wife and finally said, "I reckon we could be there. Washington, you say?"

The agents were a bit stupefied at their low-key response. "Yes, sir. We will have a plane waiting for you in Midland." The other agent interrupted. "No, I mean we will pick you up here and take you to your plane in Midland which will fly you right to Washington, D.C., and other agents will meet you there to take you right to the White House." They waited but the couple still looked uncomprehending. "You know, so you don't have to worry about how to get there or anything..." Still nothing. "And, of course, no charge to you." Finally the couple beamed.

"Well, we seen what Jackie did," his mother began. "That boy always could do anything he put his mind to."

Ernest chuckled, "If only he'd put his mind to his studies, he wouldn't be wearin' no infantry uniform." Then he realized the implications of his comment. "And, uh, we wouldn't be so damn proud of him."

The agents finished their tea and left a printed copy of the itinerary for their departure on Monday and arrival in D. C. in plenty of time for a visit that night with Jack and a tour of the White House in the morning before the ceremony. "One last thing," the shorter agent said. "We'd like to talk to Jack's friends, teachers, and so on today—just to get a sense of what kind of boy, err, man, he is."

"Well he's just a fine boy!" Jack's mother said indignantly. Ernest knew what the agents were after and offered to kindly make them a list, giving them directions to the high school and to the Oilco offices. Most of Jack's friends and even those who met-him-once had already enjoyed their 15 seconds of fame when the news media descended on Andrews, but the grilling they got from the FBI was a different story. The President did not want to be embarrassed by a tabloid story about Jack's petty crimes, sexual misorientation or anything else questionable. Jack was going to be America's hero, after all. When the FBI finally drove away, Ernest hugged his wife and they stayed that way for a long time. What a remarkable time for them all.

Chapter Thirteen

A committee of speechwriters had been at work ever since the decision was made to award Jack the medal. The joke about a camel being a horse made by a committee was never more obvious. "We need to emphasize the history of the medal," one opined while another said, "History schmistory, it's the patriotism angle." Another opted for the Texas connection, a state the President had always had a hard time with. Finally, a voice of reason won out. "It's bravery and he's not the only American who has it." Ultimately that theme would carry the day. They thought of Jack but also of the Pennsylvania plane crash victims who decided to take on their hijackers with the infamous, "Are you guys ready? Let's roll." They ended up with a speech for the President to deliver that was certain to elicit tears from even the most hardened political hack.

But it was the question of what Jack should say that had them stumped. "Did anybody find out if this kid can read?" one of the speechwriters asked in frustration. Another said, "How about this? He just says 'thank-you' and shakes the President's hand." The writers were using their delete keys almost more than any other but finally a suitably humble response was drafted and uploaded to the Teleprompter. Hopefully, they intoned, Jack would arrive in time to learn how to use the device.

While Jack was jetting across the ocean, the Hamiltons were being settled into the Willard, an old hotel a block from the White House favored by Texas oilmen, among other dignitaries; even Mark Twain wrote two books while a guest in the hotel. Ernest figured he'd see wheeling-and-dealing oilmen he knew, not that he'd approach them, even though his son was soon to be a Medal of Honor recipient.

Jack was whisked from the airfield to the Willard in a black SUV with an escort, exhausted and still frustrated. When he was shown into the suite, he was surprised to see his parents already comfortably ensconced, his dad with a bourbon and water and his mother with her proverbial sweet tea ("although I had to call down and ask for more sugar to be sent up"). After hugs, kisses and tears on the part of his mother, and another manly slap on the back from his father, Jack expressed his disappointment at being pulled away from duty. Of course, Rose was relieved, but Ernest was philosophic about it. "This is just another way your country needs you, son, so you best just do what they tell you, be a good soldier and accept the medal. What you do from that point on is up to you." His steady advice calmed Jack somewhat, but he didn't have long to enjoy it before the White House press secretary called from the lobby saying he would be up momentarily to go over Jack's speech with him. "Speech?" Jack thought. "This just gets worse and worse."

The speech, mercifully, was short and simple and the press secretary left the suite relieved that Jack could deliver it easily the next morning. Jack and his folks enjoyed a room service steak dinner and even a bottle of champagne, but it was an early night for all three. Jack didn't expect to sleep at all as wound up as he was from the flight and the nervousness at having to give a speech to the country—the world, for that matter—in the morning, but he dropped off as soon as he was in the hand-carved four-poster bed. Other than the 10-day break after boot camp when he and some of the other guys went down to New Orleans, it had been a while since he'd slept in a real bed, and certainly none as luxurious as this.

The printed itinerary said breakfast would be sent to the room at eight a.m. and that their escort would arrive an hour and a half later to take them to the White House for their tour. Both events happened to the minute. When they arrived at the White House they were greeted by myriad staffers, and Jack got a peek at the Rose Garden lawn where hundreds of chairs had already been set up facing a small stage with a dozen or so chairs in place. The Hamiltons expected that the President himself would take them on the tour, but that duty was assigned to a chatty aide who left no detail out when describing the history of every room and seemingly every piece of furniture or artwork in it. Jack would have preferred to sit quietly and think about his speech, and he knew his father would have enjoyed the same, but his mother was entranced and thrilled to see that plenty of photos were being taken ("and of course, we'll be sure that your local newspaper gets a copy of every one, just like you will").

Finally, they were shown to an anteroom leading out to the Garden. The President was ushered in and shook hands with each of them, telling them just how proud he was of Jack and how deserving he was of this ceremony. Rose looked for the First Lady but was told she was in Europe on a peacekeeping mission of some sort, but the President joked, "I imagine she's keeping the peace with Gucci or whatnot." Everyone laughed politely. A band began playing and they made their way to the stage. Jack was astounded to see the numbers of cameras, both still and television, that crowded the area in front of the stage, and the number of military brass already in place.

One of the members of the Joint Chiefs of Staff spoke briefly; Jack didn't catch his name but saw five stars on his lapels. Directly after that the President stepped to the microphone and after hearty applause began his speech, explaining that the Medal of Honor was rarely awarded and then only for acts of valor above and beyond the call of duty. He joked that the award unfortunately was often given posthumously and looked at Jack, winking, "I guess those sharks might have preferred it that way, too." He cited the illustrious company Jack was in as a recipient, including Theodore Roosevelt and his son, Theodore Roosevelt, Jr., and Arthur MacArthur, Jr. and Douglas MacArthur, another father and son. "As a Texan, Jack, maybe you can appreciate the fact that even Thomas Custer was awarded a Medal of Honor." The crowd laughed although Jack knew Custer was no

Texan. The President attached the medal, on a ribbon lanyard, around Jack's neck and stepped aside.

Finally it was Jack's turn to speak. He saluted the generals and the President and strode stiffly to the podium. Although it wasn't part of the prepared speech, he began by thanking his parents for all their support over the years and for their being present today. He barely glanced at the Teleprompter for his speech, having memorized it as soon as he had heard it yesterday. But then he went off-script, nearly sending the White House press staff into apoplexy. "Any man in my squad would have done the same thing I did." Looking directly into the cameras with his flashing blue eyes, he continued. "We know what we're fighting for — we're fighting for you, America."

The applause was thunderous. Even the President spontaneously leapt to his feet and hugged Jack, a picture that would be flashed around the world. The young Marine had become America's hero, just as the crafty senior Senator had predicted.

A lavish reception followed the ceremony. Jack, his parents and several of the high-ranking military stood in a reception line that was seemingly endless. Jack accepted the guests' praise and thanks, was able to joke with some of the men and easily charm the women. He nearly choked when Evelyn Gold, the biggest movie actress of the day, took his hand in both of hers, then pulled him closer for a breathy thank-you in his ear. This President, like many others, loved the reflected celebrity of the Hollywood elite and they were always in attendance. In addition to the actors and actresses dotting the reception area, one of the top studio executives was also watching the day's events quite closely. He sensed the immediate chemistry between Miss Gold and the soldier and felt half-ill that all cell phones had been temporarily confiscated upon entering the ceremony. He definitely had calls to make.

Chapter Fourteen

Jack was reclining in the bedroom/sitting room section of his suite, his parents having gone to bed on their side two hours earlier. He was out of his dress uniform finally and into a pair of Levis and a blue dress shirt, although that was unbuttoned and untucked. A lounge chair let him watch the twinkling lights of the nation's capital in comfort as he nursed a bourbon and water, not really his drink of choice, but it was what real men drank, according to his father. He was surprised to hear a light knock on the door and glanced at his watch, a little after ten.

He set his drink down, careful to use a coaster (his mother's voice ringing in his head). A Secret Service man was at the door, one hand held to his earphone. "Excuse me, sir," he said to Jack, "but there is someone wanting to come visit you."

"Visit me? At this hour?" Jack looked confused. "Who is it?"

"Actually, sir, the visitor prefers that it be a surprise." He hastened to add. "But, it's perfectly safe, we've checked."

"Well, if you think…"

The Secret Service spoke into some concealed microphone and Jack had to laugh—it was just like his father said, you thought you were on some television show about to be 'punked.' "All right send the surprise up." He bid Jack goodnight and disappeared back into the hallway. Jack stayed where he was and waited for the elevator door to open again. Nothing would have prepared him for who stepped out.

Evelyn Gold had a long black duster on and carried a bottle in her left hand. Her auburn hair cascaded in soft waves halfway down her back and her trademark green eyes twinkled when she saw Jack, enjoying his obvious surprise—and his open shirt.

Jack recovered his composure quicker than she would have thought possible. "That better be Jack Daniels you're packin'," he drawled.

She assumed a fake pout. "Oh, and you'd send me away if it wasn't?"

"No, but I'd damn sure call room service and make it right." He stepped back to let her enter the room. She naturally stepped to the windows to take in the view, setting the bottle of Jack down next to his half-empty drink.

"So," she turned to him, "what's a girl got to do to get a drink around here?"

Jack could feel his heart pounding but sensed she was ready to play. "What's a girl *willing* to do? Maybe that's the question," he smiled, heading for the ice bucket. "Although, in truth, it is your whiskey."

When he turned back to her, she was unbuttoning the duster. "Well, I am awfully, terribly, extremely…thirsty, cowboy," she virtually purred, drawing out every word until he thought his heart would pound right out of his chest. He didn't think his Levis would be enough to contain him either.

He crossed the room to her, swirling her drink as he went, finally dipping his index finger in. "Well, let's wet your whistle then," he said in a husky voice, drawing his finger across her lips which she opened just enough to let her tongue dart out to lick his finger, perhaps a second longer than the whiskey actually lasted. At the same time she raked her nails down his bare chest to his belt line. The sharks in the Gulf were nowhere near as terrifying.

Jack was jolted back to reality by the thought that his parents were sleeping less than fifty feet away, but that thought was banished when Evelyn at last undid the duster and slid it off her shoulders. So, Jack thought, that's what a real-life woman looks like in a teddy. Victoria's Secret's got nothin' on her. Where's the press photographer when you need him? He almost laughed to think what his friends would say if they could see him now.

Over the next several hours Jack forgot about everything—his parents, his friends, and probably his own name. Evelyn was at once aggressive then shy, not hesitating to tell him what to do and how hard to do it, then feigning innocence and letting him take charge entirely. They finally slept around three in the morning but at the first rays of daylight she was up, shrugging back into the teddy and gathering up the duster. Jack put on his most endearing look, entreating her to come back to bed, but she was insistent. "I've got to get out of here. You know damn well the press is camped outside and that's the last thing either of us needs."

He felt again like he was a cliché on a television show, asking if he'd see her again. "I don't think they'll let me bunk with you on the ship, darlin'," but sensing his disappointment, she knew she needed to leave his ego with something. "Not that I wouldn't want to...every night." She leaned over and kissed him quickly, then picked up the bedside phone. She evidently didn't have to say anything because in an instant there was a light knock on the door and she hustled out, leaving Jack stunned in her wake.

The Hollywood movie producer who had been at the White House reception and stunned by what he saw, namely Evelyn Gold flirting with the soldier, was already at work on the phones. "Herb Abraham here," he barked into the phone. "Get Mitch on the phone now." An intimated secretary apologized for the brief hold and in a moment Mitch Blanding, the leading casting director for the largest studio came on the line.

"Hey, Herb, what's up this fine morning?"

"I'll tell you what's up. I was at the White House yesterday..."

Blanding interrupted him, "Ooooh, and I'm so impressed."

"I didn't call to impress you, you ass," Abraham fired back. "I called to tell you I actually saw Evelyn Gold flirty and friendly—with a man!" He went on to describe the Medal of Honor ceremony and his absolute shock at seeing the formidable Miss Gold act like a teenage girl with her first crush.

"I wish they had that on film," Blanding chuckled, "but I can see where you're going with this." He closed up the solitaire game on his computer. "If we could find a male star she could actually get along with, it could make both of our lives a lot easier."

Abraham filled the casting director in on what he knew about Jack Hamilton, which wasn't any more than the media had shown endlessly, picking up on the "America's hero" title. Blanding agreed, "He's a good-looking kid and photogenic. That little speech of his wasn't bad, but can he act? That's the sixty-four dollar question."

"The hell it is. You know it yourself, look at all those brain-dead action stars who couldn't read a grocery list. We keep the dialogue short, the action long." Abraham was already seeing it, clearly, but Blanding was a little more reticent.

"I hate to point out the obvious, Herb, but he's in the military. His enlistment is liable to be for a couple more years. We just wait?"

"If we tell the military we need him, they'll release him. Didn't they do that for Elvis Presley or somebody?"

"No, you've got the story backwards," Blanding laughed, "and I could just see you telling some general that making a movie was more important than securing peace for America."

"Well, I'm going to work on it anyway," Abraham said grudgingly. "And I've got the perfect property for him. Remember that best-seller last year, *The Corner Saloon*? I optioned the rights to it."

"Yeah, good read," Blanding said cautiously. "You seein' him as the bartender? His name was Jack, too, wasn't it?"

"Exactly, my friend, exactly! Lots of opportunity for him to have his shirt off, and about as much dialogue as a Clint Eastwood western." He coughed excitedly. "I'm telling you. We're onto it." The two hung up with plans to do lunch later in the week.

Chapter Fifteen

The problem became, what to do with Jack? The military couldn't very well put a Medal of Honor winner on foot patrol in Afghanistan, much as Jack wanted it. Nor could they keep him in the relative safety of guard duty back in the carrier group. And yet, he still had his enlistment to fulfill. Even the President was getting pressure from all sides. "Show the American people that a soldier does just that—soldiers—and send him back to duty." From another side, "He's too valuable a public relations resource to potentially waste in combat." That led right back around to the first argument, "But look how brave that would really make him look and the mileage we could get out of it." Or, "They should have just choked him in the helicopter—that's why these awards are usually posthumous, a lot less crap to deal with."

In the meantime Jack languished at a Marine base outside of Washington, D.C., participating in routine drills and watching the "real" soldiers ship out for the game. The base specialized in helicopter operations, ironically, and every time one took off or landed, Jack's thoughts went immediately to the rescue operation. It wasn't the sight of so many soldiers dead or dying, or even the sharks that was the most vivid part of his memory; it was the rotor wash from the choppers that threatened to push Jack under every wave. He kept thinking about the power generated and thought there must be some practical use other than keeping a helicopter in flight. The "fix-it" part of him just couldn't let it go.

Finally, the powers that be came up with a plan for Jack. The public relations experts in the Marines teamed up with the White House group to invent the Home Town Hero tour in which Jack would give a speech a day, staying a week in every state, thus running the clock out on his enlistment. In his speech, usually set in a high school or community college auditorium, Jack would ask the crowd, "Are you prepared to be *your* home town hero?" A phalanx of armed forces recruiters had tables set up outside each auditorium.

Jack tired of the speech and the routine halfway into the second week and couldn't imagine putting in an entire year this way. The only perk that he could see was the number of women who waited for him after every speech. He'd never thought too much about his looks, but there had to be more to his attractiveness than just the dress uniform, he soon realized. His military "handlers" occasionally let him slip off with one of the willing women, but more often they kept Jack virtually sequestered after his appearances.

Finally, some thirty weeks into the tour, Jack came to Texas. When he stepped to the podium he was surprised to hear hecklers. Of course, they turned out to be his old buddies from the oil fields, and when Jack formally introduced them to the crowd, their heckling stopped—at least until he met them outside afterwards. "Say, bud, you're not startin' to believe your own bullshit are you?" one of the roughnecks asked him, jabbing him in the arm at the same time. They wouldn't take no for an answer and soon had Jack bundled into a pickup truck heading for a local watering hole, leaving his handlers in the dust, literally. After six or ten or who knows how many beers, Jack realized he missed the camaraderie of the roughnecks, something he never really had with his fellow soldiers. They gossiped like old women about who had left Texas to head for the boom in the Dakotas and about which local sweethearts had married or divorced. When they dropped him off at his hotel, he promised them he'd be back when his enlistment was up, and of course, they reassured him there'd always be a place for him. It was the first night in many that he slept contentedly, even though he was bothered that his parents hadn't come to any of the speeches in Texas. His father opposed U.S. involvement in what he considered another country's issues, and in one frank discussion he told Jack he viewed this much like the futility of the war in Vietnam.

The Home Town Hero tour plowed on across the states, culminating in the largest rally yet in California. The Rose Bowl in Pasadena was nearly filled to capacity on a perfect early summer day. Attendees had been asked to wear red, white and blue, and Jack thought the sight was dizzying, like a thousand American flags waving at once. He had admittedly become bored and jaded with the whole process, realizing the military was just using him, but the sheer size and enthusiasm of this crowd buoyed his spirits tremendously. Even the recruiters who had heard his speech more than two hundred times told him he had "hit it out of the park."

That evening a lavish reception was held in his honor at the famed Beverly Hills Hotel. Jack was buttoning his dress uniform jacket when he heard a soft knock at the door of his bungalow. "I'm just about ready, two secs," he yelled out, thinking it was his ever-present escort. When he finally pulled the door open Evelyn Gold nearly toppled into the room.

"So, what are you ready for?" she cooed, pulling him in for a leisurely kiss, then stepping back so he could admire her strapless navy blue gown.

"I think I liked you better in that Texas duster," Jack said to cover his surprise. "But this will do." He moved to put his arms around her, but she twirled out of his reach.

"Slow down cowboy, wouldn't do to muss up the hair and makeup before such an important evening."

He couldn't tell if she was being ironic or not but decided to take her comment at face value. "Well, apparently someone besides the local Kiwanis Club thinks I'm important," he laughed, waving at the plush bungalow. "Did they send you to escort me to dinner?"

He evidently hit a sour note because she snapped back, "Nobody *sends* me anywhere." And, even nastier, "Only common soldiers are *sent*."

Jack was shocked but wouldn't let her see it. "In that case, would you care to accompany this common soldier who is being *sent* to this big shindig in his honor?" He put his arm out for her to take it and after a moment's hesitation, she did. Without another word they walked through the lush grounds to the ballroom which was already filled with politicians, military brass, celebrities and the inevitable photographers. The Hollywood producer, Herb Abraham, was leaning on the bar talking with Mitch Blanding, the casting guru, when Jack and Evelyn made their entrance. Jack's smile lit up the room and Evelyn appeared to gaze at him adoringly, linking her arm a little more tightly through his.

"Look at that!" Herb said. "I'm telling you if they haven't already been screwing each other, they're going to. That's chemistry."

Mitch had let himself be dragged to the reception by Herb for just this reason, he realized, to see first-hand the connection between the soldier and the actress. "Well, hell, Herb, any schmuck would look good walking in with her on his arm," he teased his long-time friend. "Or, vice versa. He's a good-looking young man, all right."

"Come on, let's go introduce ourselves," Herb prodded Mitch. They finished their drinks and started to make their way through the crowd. Herb caught Evelyn's eye through the crush of people, and she immediately tugged on Jack's arm to direct him to the producer.

"What a lovely surprise," Evelyn gushed. "Jack Hamilton meet Herb Abraham and Mitch Blanding, two of Hollywood's biggest star-makers." Mitch knew in an instant that it had been anything but a surprise, but he played along, shaking Jack's hand while giving him the once-over. A good-looking guy indeed and Mitch also sensed an underlying intelligence about the man as well. A band started playing, making conversation virtually impossible, but Mitch did hand Jack his business card and implored him to call at his "earliest convenience." Mitch and Herb headed back to the bar, leaving the new glamour couple to work the room.

"I think you're right," Mitch conceded.

"About the screwing?"

"No, about using him in *The Corner Saloon*. I think he's the real deal." The two clinked glasses, but Mitch grew pensive. "Now we just have to convince him of that."

Chapter Sixteen

Jack was worn out by the time the reception finally came to a close. He'd heard, "Thank you for your service," probably a thousand times and tried to respond to each with a sincere, "It was my honor." Therefore, it came as somewhat of a relief when Evelyn stepped into a waiting limo in front of the hotel with scarcely a glance in Jack's direction, leaving him to return to his bungalow alone.

The next morning room service delivered a sumptuous breakfast, courtesy of the hotel manager, and Jack ate like a starving man, which he nearly was, having had only hors d'oeuvres at the reception. He used the time before his escort was due to arrive to sort through the business cards and scraps of paper in his jacket pockets from the night before. One woman wanted him to talk to her son, to see if Jack could "inspire" him. Several others had pressed their phone numbers into his hand while whispering into his ear a bewildering variety of sexual propositions. A handful of corporate types presented him with heavily embossed cards and urged him to call about being a motivational speaker at their next meeting. The card that intrigued him the most, however, was from Mitch Blanding at Starcast. He decided to call and find out.

Jack identified himself to the secretary at Blanding's office who immediately put him through. "It was terrific meeting you last night, Jack," Blanding began as soon as he came on the line. "You've done a great service for our country, especially for morale, and I think everyone appreciates it."

"Thank you, sir," Jack thought tiredly. More of the same. "I just wanted to call, as you suggested, and..."

Blanding cut him off. "Listen, kiddo, let's have this discussion over lunch. I'd like to bring in some other people, too." Before Jack could say another word, Blanding was leaving instructions to meet him at the Polo Lounge in the hotel at one p.m., telling him to just ask for Blanding's usual table. That left four hours for Jack to kill, so he went down to the shops in the hotel lobby hoping to buy a bathing suit and get in a few laps. The price tags on men's swim suits dashed that plan, but Jack figured, why not play the game? He called the hotel manager and just "wondered" if there was anywhere nearby where he could buy a reasonable bathing suit. Within minutes, one was delivered to his bungalow. So, Jack laughed to himself, rank does have its privileges. One interesting thing Jack had learned about being a Medal of Honor recipient was that everyone, regardless of their true rank in the military, was to salute him! So, no extra money but some interesting perks. Jack called his escort and gave him the day off.

Jack threw a towel over his shoulder and strolled out to the pool, staking out a lounge chair in the full sun, then executing a perfect dive into the deep end. Fortunately, the well-healed celebrities, or near celebrities, around the pool were more interested in themselves than in him, so no one interrupted his lap swimming. It seemed completely decadent to be lounging by a pool on a weekday morning, but Jack reflected it might be something he could get used to. He had to tear himself away from the tranquil scene to go dress for lunch. He decided a uniform wasn't necessary and just opted for khaki slacks and his favorite light blue shirt, no tie. When he strolled into the restaurant only a few minutes late he was relieved to see the other men at Blanding's table similarly attired.

Jack remembered Herb Abraham from the night before but the other introductions went by in a blur, although they were all clearly in the movie business, some as producers, "the money guys," as they referred to themselves, others in the "creative end," meaning art and set directors, it turned out. Over the next two hours they talked in a dizzying array of "points" and "market share" and "triple net," none of which Jack understood and he began to wonder why he had even been included in the group. Then one of the money guys made it clear. "So, Herb, you get Evelyn Gold and Jack here committed by the first of September, we'll get you the money, Bill will start the screenplay, Mitch finishes the casting, and Rick'll start scouting out the locations." With that he pushed back from the table, which led to another round of handshakes and the hasty departure of the others, leaving just Jack, Mitch and Herb.

"Committed?" Jack asked. "To what?"

Herb jumped in first. "We want to make a movie, and we want you to be the male lead with Evelyn being your costar." Jack burst out laughing, but Herb continued. "We've seen how you are with people, and let's face it, you and Evelyn are just on fire. You can't fake that kind of chemistry." Jack knew at least one person who could easily fake it and already had.

Mitch asked, "How much longer is your enlistment?"

Jack had a ready answer for that. "It's forty-three days," and he looked at his watch, "and three hours."

"Perfect, perfect. So by the time your enlistment is up, we'll have all the ground work in place," Mitch said, nodding at Herb. "You just need to say the word, Jack, and we'll make you a star." He folded his napkin up and placed it on the table. "You're in California a couple more days, so think about it and get back to me, say, Thursday?"

Jack felt shell-shocked and just nodded his agreement. Mitch left but Herb stayed behind. "Okay, first thing you need to get is an attorney. I'll send some standard contracts over so you can get started looking at them."

"I can't afford an attorney," Jack protested, thinking of how he couldn't even buy a bathing suit that morning.

Herb laughed. "Oh, you'll be able to afford an attorney just on the advance we're going to give you."

He pulled a cocktail napkin from under one of the glasses and scrawled a figure on it, sliding it over to Jack. "Consider this money in the bank, Jack." The figure was more than Jack would have made in the Marines if he stayed in another five years. "I'll have my secretary send you a list of entertainment lawyers we've worked with in the past, and you can pick one. Just say I referred you." He reached for the check for the luncheon and clapped Jack on the back as he stood to leave. "Don't look so excited, son. You're about to be rich and famous."

"I am famous," Jack said nervously.

"Well, so you're about to be rich," the producer said.

The next few days were hectic with Jack still having to deliver his standard recruitment speech, but now every time he gave it he imagined how it would play on the big screen. He read through the contracts. He met with an attorney. He presented to Mitch's office on Thursday and submitted to a photo session and read a few lines on camera. Every night he waited for the knock on the door of the bungalow, hoping Evelyn would at least come by to discuss their upcoming project.

At the end of the week it was time to check out of the swanky Beverly Hills Hotel and proceed to a more modest motel in Bakersfield for another round of speeches. The producer and the casting director had decided it would be best not to "leak" his upcoming venture into movie-making until his enlistment was satisfied. All three had agreed that after he was discharged he would spend a few days back in Texas then report to the studios on the first of November. The days dragged as Jack completely lost his focus on his speaking duties and found himself increasingly imagining his life as a movie star.

Chapter Seventeen

Even after his relatively short enlistment, Jack was used to following orders, but it didn't prepare him for being told exactly what to do virtually every minute he was in the movie studio. The director, an abrasive Czech whom everyone described as a "cinematic genius" seemed to take an instant dislike to Jack. Gustav Woczlaw made a Marine drill sergeant look like a pussycat in comparison, Jack thought after only a week on the set. "You must stand up straight!" Woczlaw yelled at Jack in his broken English, "but not so military. He is bartender, after all."

Jack wanted to argue that he'd read *The Corner Saloon*, and Jack, his character, had been a soldier before he ever became a bartender and old habits die hard. But he didn't. He wasn't the kind of person to do anything halfway, so every day he simply tried harder. Evelyn played the part of Juliette, an English girl forced to become a prostitute in the old West town of Virginia City, Nevada. Jack was supposed to admire her more or less from afar, according to the story, something the real Jack was grateful for. Their interactions on and off the set were becoming increasingly hostile, and Evelyn never missed a chance to say, "You're such an amateur, Jack." The way she said it left little doubt that his amateur status extended off the movie set and into the bedroom as well.

Finally one day Jack had had his fill of her attitude and answered back under his breath, "Well, playing a whore is certainly no stretch for you!" He'd come to realize that Evelyn had used him to help seal the deal for this movie and that he was also just another "notch" on her bedpost in terms of the conquests she'd made. The movie took months to film and Evelyn gradually reverted to being the notorious bitch that had made her famous in the first place. Jack read the script and counted the days until she would "die" of cholera.

But if Jack thought he was "handled" by the Marines, it was nothing in comparison to what the studio put him and Evelyn through. They were to be seen in public in the toniest places, and they were to be openly sexual with each other. The paparazzi ate up their scenes of sliding out of limos adjusting their clothing or sharing a passionate kiss outside a nightclub. Fortunately the clicking of the cameras obscured the disparaging comments the two exchanged whenever they were forced to put on such a performance.

Finally, it was "a wrap," the final scene was shot and the cast and crew popped open the obligatory champagne. Even Woczlaw pumped Jack's hand. "Is good, is very good." Jack just thought it was good that it was over, although once the movie actually hit the theaters he and Evelyn would have to endure a promotional tour for perhaps another month.

When the movie finally did come out, the critics savaged the film, singling Jack out for the most stinging criticisms. "America's hero is wooden, one-dimensional, and perhaps should consider re-enlisting—maybe in the French Foreign Legion." Evelyn didn't fare much better but when asked about it, she always deflected any criticism of her own performance to having to work with a "rank amateur." The promotional tour was canceled after only a week. Woczlaw went back to Czechoslovakia. Abraham and Blanding stopped returning Jack's calls. Jack sat in the beach house he had rented and sulked.

In Las Vegas, Bruce took Lea, Carl's former caretaker, to see the movie when it opened and both agreed it was the dullest two hours they'd ever endured. Lea had read the book and said she'd been unable to put it down, but she nearly fell asleep with her head on Bruce's shoulder during the last half-hour of the film. Bruce didn't mind. The two had seen each other off and on over the past two years, but Bruce was obsessed with getting through college as quickly as possible which didn't leave much time for dating.

Lea had thought Bruce was a sweet young man when she first met him, but her opinion of him was changing. College changes most young men, and Bruce was no exception, she realized. However, in his case it wasn't so much the influence of his professors or the pure acquisition of knowledge. Bruce was becoming cunning and manipulative, and she couldn't help wonder if she wasn't part of a larger plan.

Chapter Eighteen

Jack played *The Corner Saloon* over and over in his darkened screening room and he honestly did not see how he could have done any better. He blamed the director, the sloppy screenplay, and most of all, Evelyn whom he now referred to as the 24-carat Gold bitch. He had been used and exploited by the military, then used and exploited by the movie industry. But finally his bout of self-pity passed. He came to the realization that this had been his first real experience with failure, and it stung him terribly. He'd been a star athlete, a valued member of the biggest oil rig crew in Texas, and a war hero. But he failed at what was perhaps the most superficial job in the world. He finally had to laugh at the irony of it and when he did he knew it was time to just put it all behind him.

Instead of sequestering himself in the screening room, Jack instead took to sitting out on his deck, watching the beach goers and occasionally venturing out for a long walk along the sand. On a spectacular holiday weekend, Jack's stretch of Malibu beach was virtually solid with sunbathers although few ventured far out into the water, there being a dangerous rip current described on warning signs every twenty or so feet along the beach. Apparently not everyone believed the warnings though and suddenly Jack saw lifeguards sprinting down toward his house, all the while yelling into their radios for more help. Jack picked up his binoculars and saw the object of their concern. A boy of about twelve was being swiftly carried out in the current, battling to swim to shore instead of letting the current eventually drop him in safer waters. Jack had spent several mornings watching the lifeguards perform rescue drills in just this situation and knew they were more than capable, but when the boy was pulled out past a rocky breakwater the lifeguards looked stunned and turned back to their radios to request more help.

Within minutes, a Coast Guard helicopter swept over Jack's house and headed out toward the breakwater, following the lifeguards' hand signals. Jack was glued to his binoculars watching the life-or-death scene play out and quite a crowd had gathered on the beach below his deck. He watched as the chopper slowly lowered a basket down within the boy's reach. The pilot carefully kept the craft at an angle in an attempt to minimize the rotor wash, a phenomena Jack recalled vividly. After a seeming eternity, the basket stopped spinning long enough for the boy to catch onto it; he seemed to have just enough strength left to pull himself partway into it, then held on as the basket was retracted up into the helicopter. The crowd on the beach cheered and Jack could see the pilot give a thumbs up sign to the lifeguards.

Jack stayed out on the deck until sunset thinking about what he had witnessed. The idea that had been percolating in the back of his mind ever since his own dramatic rescue was finally taking shape and for the first time since then Jack was excited about a new direction in his life. He knew it would be a sleepless night waiting to set his plan in motion in the morning.

At 6 a.m. California time Jack took the cordless phone out to the deck to place the call to Texas. He knew Bill McAvoy would be at his desk even before the secretaries arrived so it was no surprise when he heard the gruff answer to his call. "McAvoy here, what's up?"

"Mister McAvoy, this is Jack Hamilton. I don't know if you remember me from working out in the field, but..."

"Jack, my boy, great to hear from you," McAvoy interrupted him. "How's it out there with all those movie starlets?" Clearly he hadn't heard about *The Corner Saloon's* colossal flop.

"Actually, sir, I'm ready to come back to Texas, to Oilco, if you'll have me." Jack expected a quicker response from the oilman than he got. "Sir?"

"Well, gee, Jack, our corporate PR department is pretty well set up, you know. Remember my sister, Patty? Her husband pretty much runs that show...and you know...family and all," he trailed off.

"Not to worry," Jack rushed in. "I've given all the speeches I'm ever going to." He cleared his throat and then thought, 'in for a penny, in for a pound.' "Actually, I wanted to talk to you about a position in oil development. I have an idea that I think will make you rich—richer—so I wonder if we could meet as soon as you have an hour or so." He remembered the movie director yelling at him: Sincere, say it sincere. "I wouldn't come to anyone but you with this, Bill."

The oilman was baffled but felt he owed it to this young man who had given his all for his country. "Well, sure, Jack, how about lunch at the Stockman's on Wednesday? I've got to go down to Fort Worth for a meeting anyway. Let's say about one o'clock." Jack agreed and severed the telephone connection. He had three days to flesh out his plan. He also needed a haircut and a plane reservation, things the movie studio had lined up for the past year but now he had to do on his own. It felt great.

Chapter Nineteen

Jack flew first class to Dallas-Fort Worth. His window seat afforded him a view of the vast expanse of barren land that was typical of so much of Texas, but rather than being bored with it, he found himself becoming more excited the longer he looked out the window. He had spent the last three days refining his presentation to the Oilco president and was confident he had the right combination of enthusiasm and solid engineering to sell his proposal.

The Stockman's was a landmark in Fort Worth, patronized by all the big cattle and oil men in the state and known for its huge prime beef steaks and clubby atmosphere. Jack made sure to arrive early and secure the assurance from his waiter that he, not McAvoy, would receive the check at the end of the meal. He selected a booth that would give them some privacy and also room for Jack to spread out the crude drawings he had brought for the meeting. He could see people around the room pointing to him, but no one ventured up to his table. He assumed they probably were embarrassed for him after his stint in the movies, although a year ago he would have believed they were just too awed to approach a Medal of Honor winner.

He saw McAvoy enter the dining room and slipped out of his booth to greet him. Although McAvoy had been an executive for many years, he still had the rough hands of a working man and he gave Jack a crushing handshake. His deep suntan was another indicator of how often he toured all the oil fields in his hands-on management style. Within seconds of being seated the waiter appeared with a bourbon-and-water for McAvoy who waved to several other diners in the room, then turned his full attention to Jack. "No bourbon for you?" he asked, knocking back half the drink in one swallow. "Damn, that's good stuff."

"No, sir, got to keep my wits about me when I'm talkin' to you," Jack laughed. The waiter came by with a refill for McAvoy and took their orders, a steak with all the fixins' for the oil man and a salad for Jack.

"A salad? No bourbon? You're not goin' all California fruitcake on us are you?" McAvoy boomed. The first drink was whisked away and he started on the second.

Jack blushed but had a smooth answer ready. "Well, they fed us pretty good on the plane this morning, first class and all." McAvoy seemed to accept his explanation. Before the waiter returned with the food, Jack opened a slim briefcase he'd kept below the table and brought out a file folder. "I'd like to show you what I've been thinking of," he began, but another diner came up to their table and interrupted, only to tell McAvoy a joke that even Jack had heard a million times. By then, the food had arrived and Jack slid the folder aside. McAvoy ate with gusto while Jack picked at his salad, too nervous to eat. The older man lowered his voice and leaned closer to Jack.

"So, that Evelyn Gold. She's some fine piece of tail, ain't she?"

Jack almost choked on a radish. "Oh, she's something all right." He didn't elaborate although he could tell McAvoy was hoping he would. "There's a lot of beautiful women out there, but I think our Texas gals still have 'em beat." McAvoy laughed and went back to attacking his steak.

Finally, the waiter cleared their plates and Jack was able to talk to McAvoy without interruption. "I know you've been watching this new technology going on up in the Dakotas, this fracking," Jack started, opening his file folder up on the table.

"Oh, hell, we can't do no fracking in West Texas," McAvoy sputtered. "There ain't a drop of water for 50 miles. The lakes are all dry." He looked at Jack incredulously. "Don't you watch the news, boy?"

Jack expected his response. "Sir, we don't need water. We can use something we have an abundance of in Texas—wind." He slid a drawing out of his folder showing an oil rig with something like a helicopter blade on top.

"I believe we've got plenty of hot air, that's for sure," McAvoy teased, but he leaned closer to look at the drawing. For the next two hours he let Jack patiently explain his design idea, even turning away a fourth bourbon and instructing the waiter not to bother them. Finally, the staff began changing out the tablecloths for the dinner service and the host was forced to interrupt them.

"Mr. McAvoy, sir, if you don't mind we've set up one of our smaller conference rooms so you and your guest can continue your discussions," he said and began to help gather up the papers spread across the table. When he saw the drawings Jack and McAvoy had made on the white linen tablecloth, he barely flinched and folded that up as well, leading the two men to an oak-paneled meeting room with a conference table big enough for eight.

Jack was just at the point of making his request. "Sir, what I would propose is this…"

McAvoy looked at his watch and interrupted him. "Hell's bells, I got to be at that fundraising banquet in about a half-hour, barely time enough to get to the hotel and into a suit." He knew Jack was frustrated and tried to convince him to come to the banquet, but Jack declined.

"I told my folks I'd drive up there tonight. My mom's doing poorly and my father's having quite a time with her."

"Well, I'm surely sorry to hear that. Your folks are good people," McAvoy said, his hand on Jack's shoulder. "You let us know if there's anything we can do." He started to step away then turned back, "And, Jack, I think you're onto something. You call me as soon as you get your folks settled and we'll talk some more." Jack's face lit up and his shoulders finally relaxed.

Chapter Twenty

It seemed almost as if Jack's mother were waiting for him to return home in order to let herself pass. On the second morning he was home, Jack's father came into the kitchen where Jack was making coffee. "Well, she's gone," Ernest said with a hitch in his voice. "In the middle of the night she just held my hand and that was that." Jack looked at his father and thought he had collapsed into himself, looking half the size he had only the day before. His parents had been together a long time, having been high school sweethearts, and Rose's loss might prove too much for Ernest to handle.

Jack was at a loss for words but hugged his father, something he couldn't recall doing more than once or twice in his life, then went into the bedroom to say goodbye to his mother. The appropriate authorities were summoned and Jack spent the rest of the day going through his mother's phone book calling friends and neighbors. By late afternoon the house was full of people, all bearing food and condolences. Ernest sat in his favorite chair with a far-away look on his face and said little to anyone, mutely accepting their sympathy.

People from several surrounding towns attended the funeral, overflowing the Methodist church where Jack's parents had married. Oilco sent the largest flower arrangement although only a vice president of the company was in attendance, along with a few of Jack's roughneck buddies. After the service, however, the vice president made his way to Jack and apologized for McAvoy's absence; he was in Washington, D.C. working on some important legislation, but he did want Jack to call him as soon as his family duties would allow.

A week later Jack was shown to McAvoy's office on the twenty-fourth floor of the Oilco building with its commanding view of...nothing, just more of West Texas. After expressing his condolences, McAvoy got right to the point. "I talked to some of our engineers and they think your idea of using pressure alone, generated by those wind turbines, might be enough to accomplish the same thing as the fracking they're doing now."

"I believe it will, sir," Jack said eagerly. When he thought back to the day of his famous rescue at sea, it was always the power of the rotors that came back to him, not the sharks or the faces of the men he saved, and those he didn't. "I'd like to tell you my proposal, if I may, and we'll see where we stand." For the next half-hour Jack outlined his desire for Oilco to give him control over a grouping of perhaps three oil rigs that were determined to be "played out," so that Jack could put his technology in motion. He had already talked to his roughneck friends and identified a likely site with a grouping of three abandoned rigs. At the end he pledged McAvoy. "We'll split any oil that results fifty-fifty." He stood and extended his hand toward the older man. McAvoy shook it solemnly then reached in his desk for a bottle of Jack Daniels.

"So, now is it time for a bourbon?" It must have been because the two clinked glasses displaying the Oilco logo. All the legal mumbo-jumbo took another week to finalize, but at last Jack was ready to head out into the field to begin testing his idea. He'd used the week to put a skeleton crew together, particularly since he was financing the up-front costs, although he was free to salvage used equipment from the oil fields and "tweak" things together like he always had.

Jack continued to live at home, thinking he was helping his father, and besides he had no social life other than the occasional card games with the other workers. This time he took to wearing the jack of spades in the band of his cowboy hat and easily regained his nickname of Black Jack Hamilton.

His father, however, seemed reticent to talk to Jack about his project, and Jack knew he still harbored a deep distrust about Jack's 'promotion,' as he called it, of the war in the Middle East. Therefore, it surprised Jack when his father started in one night, "So, seems to me you pump all the pressure in the ground, it's got to release itself somewhere."

"When the oil starts to move, dad, that'll release the pressure," Jack started to explain.

His dad waved his hand dismissively. "Well, I guess you figure you know." With that he dragged himself out of his recliner. "I'm going to bed." When Jack left for the oil field the next morning his father was still in bed, a habit he'd developed just lately, so Jack thought nothing of it. Later that day, however, Howard Jones, his father's best friend drove out to the rig. He walked slowly toward Jack, removing his hat as he approached. "I'm afraid I've got some bad news for you son," he said slowly. Jack knew instinctively what the man would say but let him continue. "I went by to get your dad for Rotary this morning, but when he didn't come to the door, I went around back," and he sighed deeply. "He's gone, Jack. Your good old dad has passed." He stood there in the dust waiting for Jack's reply, until finally he just put his hand on Jack's shoulder and the two stood there in silence.

After a moment, Jack mumbled his thanks and said he'd be heading on back to the house to put things in order. Howard said he'd join him in a while; he wanted to go to the Rotary meeting and let the other men know. So for the second time in as many months, Jack found himself organizing a funeral, and again the Methodist church was full to overflowing.

The palpable sadness seemed to linger in the small town for days afterward. Jack was almost grateful to escape into the long days of back-breaking work it took for him to assemble the wind-driven turbines that he hoped would unlock untapped reserves of oil. In the back of his mind though, Jack wished his father had lived long enough to see this dream become reality. His father had visited the oil rig once but left shaking his head and without saying a word to Jack. But then, Jack rationalized, his father had been a feed store manager, not an oil man.

Nearly two months later the day finally arrived when Jack could at last begin his "air-fracking" venture. Several of the Oilco executives visited Jack's rig 19 and watched as the massive turbines began to turn and compressed air and other gases were forced down into the previously-abandoned oil shaft. Jack had climbed partway up the rig and waited to be bathed in a gusher of oil. His 100-watt smile was easily visible by the crowd of onlookers.

Within seconds a fireball lit up the dull Texas sky and customers in the diner five miles away felt the explosion. The pressure from the air and gasses had blown the rig straight up in the air and its remnants rained down on the crowd, killing two people and injuring dozens of others. When the debris settled ambulance sirens could be heard in the distance, everyone in town knowing there had been a major disaster in the oil fields.

Jack, or what was left of him, was found hundreds of yards from the ruined oil rig. His lower leg was discovered impaled on a cactus some twenty feet from his body. "Ah, leave it be," the ambulance crewman said as another tried to pry it free. "Won't do him no good now." Several of Jack's charred fingers were found still clutching part of the rigging ladder. Jack held onto consciousness long enough to be relieved his father hadn't lived to see him fail again.

Chapter Twenty-One

Bruce watched the spectacular news coverage of the burning oil rig and thought back to that day in the student union at the University of Nevada. He and another student had watched Jack's daring rescue, the other student calling him the luckiest man on earth. Well, Bruce thought, the luckiest man's luck sure ran out today. But it hadn't entirely.

When the doctor on duty at the small Andrews hospital in town realized who had been wheeled in on a gurney, he immediately requested a medical helicopter transport. "America's hero is not dying on my watch," he told the EMS crew standing by Jack's stretcher. "I'm calling the trauma center in Dallas and telling them to expect a challenge." The medics who had transported Jack to the home-town ER doubted Jack would make it even partway to Dallas, but it wasn't their position to challenge the local doctor. They had already started a fluid bolus en route to the hospital and dosed Jack heavily with morphine. Jack had second- and third-degree burns over most of his remaining limbs and torso, and not even his mother would have recognized his face, also a charred, blistered catastrophe.

Jack's luck, what little of it remained, put the chopper in nearby Midland instead of at its home base in Dallas, so it arrived within just minutes to Andrews. The expert crew scooped Jack up and were underway in seconds, having already been apprised of his identity. Jack sensed more than heard or saw the helicopter lifting off, thinking just how ironic that was. The helicopter nurses gave him more morphine and he drifted back into unconsciousness and remained that way throughout the flight.

Even before the helicopter landed in Dallas, Jack had already become something of a political football, with the hospital administration arguing that he should be transferred immediately to a military hospital and the doctors arguing against it. "This young man barely has a chance of surviving," the head trauma surgeon argued, "and we'll be decreasing that chance to nothing if we keep flying him around the country." He didn't say it out loud but he was thinking, "And, we'll do a damn sight better job than any VA hospital will."

Finally a low-level admissions clerk put the issue to rest. "Holy crap, you should see what kind of insurance he has!" Jack was technically still under contract to the movie studio, which "optioned" him for five years. In so doing they also took out a multi-million dollar insurance policy on him in case anything should happen while filming the sometimes dangerous stunts.

In the weeks to come Jack would see the irony in that as well. "I'll bet they wish I'd fallen off a horse and hit my head on a rock," he thought to himself. "They wouldn't have had to finish that turkey of a movie." He would not have been surprised to see Herb Abraham himself enter his hospital room in hopes of pulling the plug on Jack.

When Jack's helicopter landed in Dallas, the trauma surgeon had already assembled a full team waiting on the tarmac—orthopedics, plastic surgery, cardiology, pulmonology and anesthesia. An operating room was ready and time had been booked every day for the next month in the hyperbaric chamber to speed Jack's wound healing—provided he survived that long. The triage process basically consisted of the trauma surgeon trying to determine what could be saved of the grievously injured former soldier. "His left eye is not salvageable," he dictated to a scribe. "Half of his left leg is gone. We have to modify that stump and control the bleeding, debride out any bone chips, create a solid flap coverage." He looked at Jack's left arm. "I think we can take it off right below the elbow, give him some chance at a decent prosthesis down the road." But overall he stood back and looked at Jack. "That is one messed up son of a bitch."

Chapter Twenty-Two

Jack endured agonizing surgery after surgery, and the burn treatment was a hundred times worse than anything he could have imagined. His face was a crazy quilt of skin grafts, puckering, suture lines, darker areas and lighter pigments. But, he thought wryly, at least shaving wasn't an issue for the moment. Some of the nurses tried flirting with him to cheer him up, but most tried to avoid looking at him at all. For all of the work by the plastic surgeons, Jack still looked essentially like a monster, which is also what he felt like for having killed two roughnecks that day on the rig and injuring the spectators, some of them quite badly.

The only thing that took his mind off the responsibility he felt was the dreaded physical therapy sessions three times a day. The therapists told him that the skin grafts could not be allowed to tighten up and they encouraged him to keep his muscle tone intact as much as possible. They pushed, pulled and twisted him until he was a quivering mess pleading for more pain meds. And then they came back and did it all again three hours later and three hours after that. It went on for months during which time Jack was fitted with a prosthetic leg that he found chafed his stump and dragged when he tried to walk. The orthopedists had been able to save his elbow and provided him with another prosthesis, this one being a metal claw where his left hand had been. He was thankful for being right-handed, but again the therapists insisted he learn to use the claw. He spent hours picking up marbles and rolling balls across a table.

And, of course, there was the weekly meeting with the hospital psychiatrist. Jack would have traded three hours of wound debridement for three minutes with the man. He doggedly encouraged Jack to "use this time wisely to develop insight." Insight into what Jack wasn't sure and the psychiatrist always gave him a vague reply, usually in the form of another question. "Why do you think you feel that way?" he would ask Jack if Jack so much as divulged even one emotion, so he stopped talking to the doctor entirely and remained mute while the man flipped idly through his chart. Mercifully, after a month he no longer stopped at Jack's room.

Given Jack's schedule of treatments and his overall attitude, it wasn't surprising that he received few visitors. When Bill McAvoy's big frame filled the doorway one afternoon Jack couldn't help but be surprised. McAvoy flinched noticeably when he looked at Jack but tried to cover it up with a hearty, "Hey, son! They treating you okay here?"

"Oh, yeah, we're havin' a grand old time," Jack said sarcastically, then regretted speaking so harshly to the oil man who had backed him and suffered losses — financial and personal — as well. "I'm sorry, sir. It's a tough deal, I'll tell you."

McAvoy pulled up the only chair in the room, set his cowboy hat on the end of Jack's bed, then leaned forward, elbows on his knees. "So, you given any thought to what you're going to do when they cut you loose of this place?"

Jack laughed for the first time in months. "Oh, I expect I'll find a circus somewhere that needs a new freak." The bout of laughter had pulled at the facial skin grafts and Jack sought the morphine pump button to soothe the pain. McAvoy reached it first and gently pulled it out of Jack's reach, infuriating Jack who said nothing. "I don't imagine you're here to offer me my job back, are you?" he snarled. "Or maybe you'd like me to be the new face of the oil industry, go on a speaking tour denouncing the dangers of fracking?" He wanted to weep from the pain and frustration but was determined not to show any of that to McAvoy who apparently was going to let him have his rant and get it over with.

Jack sighed and closed his eye, hoping McAvoy would take the hint and leave. But the Texas tycoon was staying put. "Actually, when you get done with your little pity party, as my wife likes to call it, maybe you can think seriously about what I *am* going to offer you." When Jack said nothing, McAvoy continued. "I have been approached by a man who wants to meet you and asked me to make that happen. I don't know him personally but I did some askin' around and apparently he's on the up and up." At this point he leaned forward and put his hand gently on Jack's shoulder. "I know you've got a lot to be sorry for, but you're still a solid young man and you've got a long life ahead of you that won't be spent in this hospital bed."

Jack realized McAvoy wouldn't leave until he'd said everything he came to say. "Okay, you've got my attention. Why anyone would want to meet me unless it's another lawyer is beyond me. So, what gives?"

"His name is Vince Ciriglio and actually he's waiting downstairs in the coffee shop for me to give him a call and tell him to come up. You okay with that?"

"I'm not really in any position to resist," Jack said, then a little lighter, "but just tell him I don't have my makeup on."

McAvoy stepped out into the hall to make the call, releasing the morphine pump button to Jack's control. Jack eyed it but didn't depress the plunger. He'd see what this guy wanted and then decide.

A few minutes later McAvoy returned to the hospital room, trailing a swarthy man with a stocky build and a head full of wavy black hair. He had a light gray suit on with a black shirt and no tie, a riot of chest hair showing at the unbuttoned collar. He approached Jack and didn't bat an eye at his appearance, extending his hand for a solid handshake. Even people who had been warned about Jack's condition still couldn't help reacting at the sight of him, but Ciriglio seemed unfazed. "Vince Ciriglio," he said, still pumping Jack's hand. "I'm pleased to meet you, young man." At this point McAvoy stood to leave, vacating his seat for Ciriglio.

"Jack, it was good seeing you," McAvoy said. "You keep in touch now." Jack figured it would be the last he ever saw of his oil field partner.

A nurse stopped by the room to check Jack's vital signs and the various drains, then left with a warning to Jack's new visitor that he should limit his stay to another ten minutes. Ciriglio winked at Jack. "And the docs think they run these joints!" Jack knew better than to laugh again without the additional morphine. "So in ten minutes, let me tell you who I am," Ciriglio began. "I'm originally from New York, Little Italy, obviously," he said expansively, "but for the last five years I've been in Vegas. You been?" Jack nodded yes and Ciriglio continued. "So, I have been what you call 'facilitating' various gaming operations for my friends, who in turn give me a share of their operations." Now he leaned closer to Jack. "But I think those days are over. It's time for me—and you—to expand into our own enterprise." His eyes lit up and he became even more enthusiastic. "I'm telling you, Jack—can I call you Jack? I'm telling you, Vegas is ripe for the picking and we are the people to pick it."

Jack finally managed to get a word in. "I don't know why you would think I know anything about Las Vegas or what goes on there." With a grimace he said, "Apparently the only thing I've ever done successfully is pull soldiers out of the ocean."

Ciriglio waved Jack's comments away. "Oh, that's all in the past. You had your tough spots, everyone does…"

"You call *this* a tough spot?" Jack said incredulously.

"Okay, that's not what I meant, sincerely," the Italian continued, gesturing with his hands. "No, I mean you think big and that's what we need, a guy who isn't afraid to think big and put his money where his mouth is." He spread his hands out before Jack. "You and me have got what it takes!"

Jack pushed the morphine plunger furiously. "I'm sorry, Mr…?"

"Just call me Vince, Vince Ciriglio," his visitor jumped in. "Look, I see you're tired and I've overstayed my welcome, but I'm going to come back and see you soon my friend." By the time he stood up to leave, Jack was already asleep.

Chapter Twenty-Three

Vince was back at Jack's bedside every day for the next week, patiently explaining just what he wanted from Jack and what Jack would get in return. He was relentless in his pursuit, even wheeling Jack to his therapy sessions and continuing to talk to him there. He started every sentence, it seemed, with, "The thing is…" and then went on to explain 'the thing' with hand gestures that made him look like a symphony conductor on fast-forward.

"The thing is, Jack, to think big, that's the thing," Vince droned on while Jack struggled to walk with his new prosthesis between parallel bars, Vince on one side, the therapist on the other. "I'm not telling you anything new, I'm sure, because you're a big thinker, Jack." He laughed and forgetting Jack's condition, slapped him on the back. "Okay, so you're no engineer, but you're a big thinker and that's what works in Vegas." The remark stung almost as much as the slap. The therapist laughed unwillingly. The staff had come to appreciate the wildly gesticulating Italian and his grandiose speeches because they were in such sharp contrast to Jack's dour moods.

Vince had explained to Jack that he and some "other friends" owned a small hotel in Las Vegas positioned right at the center of The Strip, but what they really needed was a casino, and for that they had to obtain a gaming license from the State of Nevada. "The thing is, this is where you come in, Jack," Vince beamed and spread his arms. "You're still America's hero, you're squeaky clean reputation-wise, and you'd be a shoe-in to get a license." Jack looked dubious. "Me and my friends, see, we've had a few little 'misunderstandings' you might say, that could make it difficult to get that license."

"So, I'd just be a front man for a bunch of thugs?" Jack said in a surly tone he'd developed since being in the hospital.

Vince appeared to clutch his chest. "Thugs? Thugs? Oh, we certainly don't merit such a description." He appeared offended for the moment but his irrepressible enthusiasm came back. "No, none of us has even so much as a felony conviction that stuck. We're just from the wrong neighborhood, capiche?"

"I don't *capiche* anything," Jack replied, still testy. "I don't know the first thing about running a casino or a hotel or even a roulette wheel." He seemed ready to collapse between the bars so the therapist put a wheelchair behind him. "And the way my luck has gone we'd be the first casino in history where the house *lost* money."

Vince knew it was time to stop for the day, but he couldn't leave without one parting shot. "I don't see you taking a lot of other meetings with interested parties. This is where you could make your mark, Jack, really make your mark." He winked at the therapist and blew a kiss to the nurse standing by. "I'll be back, Jack. You think about it. Make your mark."

The boom in Las Vegas had allowed many people to make their mark, and one of them was Bruce. Not only had he graduated from UNLV without any student debt, he came out with a small bundle of money from Carl's inheritance and his own shrewd investments. He'd read every book and magazine he could get his hands on about making money and it became his total focus. His caregiver days were well behind him, but he hadn't forgotten what got him started. He still kept in touch with Lea, not because he thought she was a lovely girl, which she was, but because she came from a big family of caregivers, and those were just the people he needed.

Bruce's first business venture was a nursing home out in Pahrump. The dilapidated eight-bedroom home was actually just a collection of double-wide trailers arranged around a small central courtyard. Bruce had his suspicions that the place might have previously been a whorehouse, being in a county of Nevada where such ventures were legal, but it suited his purpose and it was cheap. Bruce had a business partner, a former accounting major like himself, Greg Nelson, who had the scruples of an alley cat and had mostly cheated his way through school. Bruce thought he was the perfect partner for what he had in mind, and he knew Greg was no match for himself in business savvy.

"I'm sure as hell not living out there," Greg said when he and Bruce toured the facility. "And I don't see you out here either," he challenged Bruce. The town was about fifty miles from Las Vegas and was basically a gateway to Death Valley and home to a half-dozen correctional facilities.

"No need to," Bruce replied with his Cheshire cat smile. "If we throw a few more trailers out here, Lea's family will jump at the opportunity for cheap housing and jobs." He added, "Trust me, those people's standards are pretty low."

Buying the future nursing home proved to be the easy part of the new venture. Finding the people to put in it was another matter, but Bruce felt certain he had the finesse to carry it off by simply reconnecting with his former emergency department workers. He and Greg left the trailer complex and went to the town's only golf course bar to sketch out a plan. Greg was in favor of finding clientele on death's doorstep, collecting their Social Security benefits, and then not reporting their deaths, but that was too far a leap into fraud for Bruce. He knew there were other ways to work the system.

Chapter Twenty-Four

True to his word, Vince was back at Jack's bedside the next day. "So, whaddya think? You ready to come out to Vegas and check this thing out?" He didn't wait for Jack to answer but plowed on. "Here's the thing. We've got a chance to buy a whole city block right in the middle of The Strip, right next to our hotel, and bang, we're ready to build the swankiest casino Vegas has ever seen—and you'd be the President of it."

"What do I put up besides my sterling reputation?" Jack asked sarcastically.

"Well," Vince replied thoughtfully. "We'd like you to have some skin in the game." He laughed at his own poor joke which only made Jack's scowl deepen. "I know you've got some money left over from the studio deal and your stay here isn't costing you a dime, so I figure," and he appeared to actually do just that, "I figure a couple hundred grand for starters." Then he added, "And you sell that place in Texas." Vince normally stood and paced when he talked to Jack, but he pulled up the chair and lowered his voice. "Here's the thing. The real money is coming from back East, but it's clean, really."

So, after a week of Vince's badgering, haranguing, entreating, cajoling and finally almost pleading, Jack gave in. In truth, he had nowhere else to go. He was a pariah in Texas and a laughingstock in California. He had no family and very few friends left. In retrospect, it seemed like collusion to Jack, but this was the moment his primary doctor sailed into the room. "Good news, Jack, I think we've done everything we can for you, so you're good to go."

"You mean you've done everything you can *to* me," Jack said grudgingly.

The doctor started to reply, "Well, you've got to admit..." but Vince cut him off by slapping him on the back, thanking him for everything, then turning him toward the hospital room door. Jack thought Vince might actually drag the doctor out of the room if it came to it.

"So, here's the thing, Jack, I'll go get you some clothes and..."

"Please, no shiny suits and dark shirts," Jack said, actually laughing with the vision of leaving the hospital dressed like Vince.

"Oh, fine, now you're the fashion expert, too," Vince quipped. "I guess if I come back with a dress you'll wear it if you want to blow this joint." They made plans for Vince to come back after lunch during which time Jack could make the rounds to say goodbye to his therapists and nurses and Vince could shop and charter a plane for their flight to Las Vegas, plus let his partners know that Jack was on board with their plan.

When Vince returned with boot-cut levis to accommodate Jack's prosthesis and a western shirt, Jack was relieved but challenged at having to dress himself for the first time in months. Vince stood back but was finally too impatient to watch him struggle. As he buttoned up Jack's shirt he tried to make light of it. "Next time we'll get those pearly-looking snaps, paaardner." He even had a pair of sunglasses for Jack. So, the unlikely pair left the hospital and stepped into a cab for the short ride to a private airfield where a Gulfstream was waiting. Jack felt almost giddy at being out at last but said nothing to Vince about it. He was still filled with trepidation about what awaited him in Las Vegas.

The flight was less than four hours and when they touched down at McCarran International Airport they again went to a section of the field reserved for private aircraft and deplaned to a waiting dove-gray limo. The driver snapped to attention as soon as he saw Vince and rushed forward to grab his baggage. Jack saw him stealing covert glances in his direction, trying not to openly stare. "Well, get used to it," he said to himself.

The driver exchanged a few words with Vince on the tarmac, then held the door open for him and nodded to see that Jack was already settled in the back seat. Even those few minutes outdoors was agony, Jack found, as the sun hit skin grafts that were still very sensitive, making him feel like he was being burned all over again. The fact that he would be living in a casino where daylight is never seen looked more attractive by the minute, he thought with some grim satisfaction.

As the sleek limo glided up The Strip, Bruce and Greg watched it pull abreast of their battered Chevy Camaro. "You look at that buddy," Bruce nudged Greg. "It won't be long before that's how we're traveling."

"From your mouth to God's ears," Greg said sardonically. "In the meantime, we've got to go shopping for swamp coolers and hospital beds. Oh, and bed pans, let's not forget the bedpans." Greg knew how Bruce had come by his little "nest egg" and they both felt if it had worked once, there was every chance it work again—if they could only find the right patient.

The limo pulled under the porte cochere of the hotel and although the car's darkened windows blunted some of the neon, Jack could tell it was flashy and gaudy, nothing classy about it. But, true to Vince's description there was a large empty parcel next door with a freshly-painted sign: "Las Vegas' largest casino here soon brought to you by AHG, pioneers in gaming."

"AHG?" Jack asked Vince.

Vince beamed. "America's Hero Group. What did I tell you, baby! It's all happening."

Two burly security guards stood ready to open the front doors as Jack and Vince approached, the limo driver having already handed over their baggage. Jack was forced to make his way through the entire length of the casino to a mirrored elevator at the far end. Seeing himself in a full-length mirror for the first time nearly brought him to his knees, but thankfully the doors slid open after only a few seconds' wait and they stepped into the cocoon, away from the casino's clamor. Vince used a key to unlock access to the top floor and when the elevator glided to a stop it opened directly into a suite. Jack was immediately drawn to the floor-to-ceiling windows overlooking The Strip and thought back to that night in Washington, D.C. where he gazed at the nation's capital building in awe. Different sights, he thought, and certainly different times.

Chapter Twenty-Five

While Bruce and Greg were shopping for hospital beds and customers to put in them, Vince and Jack were shopping for thousands of tons of steel, concrete, and myriad other building materials. And there were the contractors and subcontractors to deal with, hundreds of them. Vince did all the up-front, in-person negotiating while Jack did much of the research into pricing, timing of delivery, and inspections. Vince kept a steel lockbox in his desk filled with envelopes containing varying amounts of hundred dollar bills, all to "grease the skids," as he put it. Jack didn't see much of the other partners, which Vince said was "just as well."

Before construction could really begin, however, AHG had to secure a gaming license from the State of Nevada. Jack had completed the voluminous paperwork of the application and learned that one aspect of his past considerably sped up the process — the fact that the FBI had once thoroughly vetted him before he received the Medal of Honor. His life had basically been an open book since then, being on display in Hollywood as he was, and then everyone watching the devastating event in the West Texas oilfields.

A hearing date was set for which they would have to travel to the Gaming Commission offices in Carson City. Jack could think of nothing else as the day approached, and that morning when it was time to leave for the airport, he finally told Vince he couldn't do it. He could not let himself be stared at—and of course, the media would show pictures of his formerly handsome, well-muscled, brightly-smiling self next to the disfigured thing he had become. Vince tried every kind of reassurance but finally realized nothing was going to get Jack out of his hotel suite.

While he was pleading with Jack, however, he had an inspiration just watching the technicians at work in the suite installing a closed-circuit monitoring system that would allow Jack to oversee the entire hotel and the hopefully soon-to-be construction next door. He went into another room and busily started working the phones. His first call went to the Gaming Commission offices where, fortunately, he had become friendly with the main administrative assistant. "Karen, doll, here's the thing," he began brightly. "You know Jack went through a terrible, terrible trauma, and he just hasn't recovered enough to go out in public." Karen protested that they were to be in front of the commission in less than three hours. But Vince turned on his charm. "So, we're wondering, could we do this thing via closed-circuit television?" He could hear her thinking about how that might happen. "And, let me go one better. How about if we get a sitting judge to come here to Jack's suite, and he can verify that Jack's who he says he is, all that, you know?" Now he had to come up with a judge on a moment's notice! While Karen had him on hold, he called a pit boss at another nearby casino. Was there perchance a judge who liked to gamble, maybe a little too much? He got a name immediately, scribbled it on a piece of paper and told the pit boss he'd be by later to take care of him.

Karen came back on the line. "I've spoken to Commissioner Nulty. This is all highly unusual, but he believes in supporting the industry, as you know, so…"

"So it's a deal. Great, great. We'll have the judge here at one and the television feed set up." He warned Karen though, "No other media in the room. This is for the Commissioners' eyes only." She indicated she understood then put another assistant on to ask about how to set up the television on their end. Vince was going to pull this out after all. There would have been hell to pay from the partners otherwise. He went back into Jack's room to tell him the good news, only to hear him retching in the adjacent bathroom. Vince could only shake his head and think about the hell his new friend and partner had been through already in his young life.

The judge arrived a few minutes before the televised interview was to start and accepted a vodka neat from Vince. Jack hadn't emerged from his bedroom yet but yelled out to Vince that he was "in control." When he did come out the judge took a larger swallow of his vodka to mask a grimace, but he stood and shook Jack's hand in a friendly way, assuring him he was happy to help out. "All I had was more drug court this afternoon," he explained, "and you can imagine what a boring waste of time that is." He looked around the suite and out at The Strip, far less glamorous in the daylight. The technician clipped a small microphone on Jack's shirt, then gestured him to a chair near the window where the camera had already been set up. After a few tests of the equipment, the technician showed Jack how his face would be blurred during the proceedings. Jack tried to joke that he would have been more comfortable with a gunnysack over his head, but the mood in the room remained serious.

The interview began with the Commissioners in Carson City introducing themselves. The judge then introduced himself and then Jack and indicated he had indeed confirmed Jack's identity as that of Jack Ray Hamilton, a bona fide partner in the AHG Corporation. Commissioner Nulty restated what he had told his assistant earlier, "Mr. Hamilton, this proceeding is highly unusual, but the Commission exists to support and protect our very crucial gaming industry, and so in that spirit we were willing to accommodate your desire for protection from the media." He chuckled a bit. "Anyone can understand that."

Another Commissioner whose name Jack had already forgotten took over. "Our main interest in this proceeding is to confirm that you are not under any undue influence from any party to seek this license." He paused for emphasis and leaned toward the camera. "We are particularly vigilant in keeping any organized crime interests out of our state." He shuffled through some papers. "I do see that you have completely cleared the FBI investigation and our own internal investigators are satisfied with your background." At this point he, too, laughed. "My gosh man, you haven't even had a speeding ticket that we can find!"

It was Jack's turn to laugh. "With all due respect, sir, for most of my life I haven't owned a car capable of achieving a speeding ticket." Even Vince was surprised at Jack's attempt at levity, but he quickly turned more serious. "I appreciate you helping me today, and I can assure you I take the proceeding very seriously. My future depends on it and I am very desirous of being a solid, law-abiding member of our gaming industry." There ensued a number of questions about the financing of the proposed casino, all of which Jack handled easily, having been coached for hours on end by Vince.

In the end the vote was unanimous to award an unrestricted gaming license to AHG Corporation, held in the name of corporate president Jack Hamilton. The Commission Chairman solemnly closed the session by speaking directly into the camera to Jack. "I'm sure I speak for all of us in wishing you well and thanking you for your service to America. Good luck, son." The light went off on the camera and Vince whooped in delight, although at least this time he remembered not to slap Jack on the back.

Chapter Twenty-Six

Bruce and Greg finally had their nursing home in Pahrump more or less outfitted and staffed, and they had passed the very minimal State requirements for licensure. It surprised Bruce a little to see just how easy it was to find doctors willing to put their name on the staff list. Some of them had previous drug or disciplinary problems and others had questionable degrees from medical schools in the Caribbean or the Bahamas. There were nurses who had let some of their critical certifications lapse and were uninterested in pursuing the continuing education needed to reinstate them. In short, there was a virtually unlimited pool of potential employees able to provide the minimum level of care allowable, not that anyone cared, a fact Bruce and Greg were counting on.

When Bruce called on emergency room triage nurses or on hospital social workers, he was able to project the most benevolent, caring, competent picture. He often referred back to the care he provided Carl and what a "pivotal" experience it had been in his life, although his listeners had no idea what he was really referring to, namely, inheriting Carl's estate. "We really want to provide perhaps end-of-life care to those poor souls who have no family to look after them and are otherwise just at anyone's mercy," Bruce would say with such sincerity. "We'll work with whatever meager resources they have and provide them with the best personal care possible." He'd smile and perhaps place his hand over the triage nurse's or social worker's hand. It worked like a charm. The hospitals were all too happy to discharge these kinds of patients to Bruce's facility. And yes, Bruce would transport them himself.

Lea had thought she and Bruce might eventually become a true couple, but when she saw how contemptuous he was of the helpless patients and how dismissive he was with the staff (many of whom were her family members), she was happy she had stayed at her hospital job in Las Vegas. "I'm just a happy little farmer," he'd boast to her, "waiting to harvest my dying crop," and then he'd bray like a donkey at what he considered his clever pun. If patients survived their stay at what Bruce and Greg decided to call Pahrump Place, some were often grateful enough to bequeath their entire estates to Bruce. In other cases, Bruce used the legal machinery to simply take what remained, using the same method he had learned with Carl—establish custody and just await their deaths. Greg grew restive with the plan that might net them $10,000 or $20,000 a month, barely enough to pay expenses, and certainly not enough to make them rich. They just needed that one big fish, Bruce would reassure him. "We're just betting on the come, baby."

Bruce had learned other ways to work the system, too. He put Greg to work scouting every state and federal program that had the potential to bring money to Pahrump Place. He secured hundreds of thousands of dollars in job-training grants designed to produce more certified nursing assistants. There were research grants to study any number of aspects of aging. The staff doctors simply filled out the forms, and forms and forms and forms.

While Bruce and Greg were hoping to snag just one rich benefactor, Jack and Vince were looking for a dozen. While they had been assured of big East Coast money, it was only a fraction of what was needed to build the casino—and it all had strings attached. Every time another few million was needed, Vince was on the plane, hat in hand. He'd come back and complain to Jack. "They're breakin' my balls, I'm tellin' ya." He was forced to give up points, or ownership shares, in the casino and finally conceded to Jack. "I swear. We'll be lucky to own any of this when it's done." Jack wasn't particularly surprised but just had to hope, as Vince did, that once the doors opened they could buy back at least some of the points. "Otherwise, we'll be parking their damn cars!" Vince lamented.

Jack had come to respect and admire Vince, almost looking at him as the older brother he never had. His enthusiasm never seemed to flag and he could charm even the toughest contractors and union guys, plus he held their ever-growing number of partners in a cautious truce. Vince was about twenty years older than Jack, had been married twice but had no children. His eyes lit up whenever one of his nieces or nephews called him, and he promised each of them that they would get the best seats by the pool whenever it opened. He and Jack had established a routine whereby he would come to Jack's suite around six in the evening and enjoy a cocktail or two, then wait to accept Jack's room service dinner delivery. He was never able to get the increasingly reclusive young man to go out to dinner, but at least this seemed somewhat social. Jack realized one such night that he had no idea where Vince lived nor what he himself did for dinner. In the mornings, Vince would often come by the suite and discuss what their respective projects should be for the day.

Jack found that although Vince praised him for being a big thinker, what he really enjoyed and was good at was the minutiae, the thousand small details that went into even one small segment of building the massive casino resort. He didn't mind spending hours on the phone asking question after question. "Why should we have that type of palm tree?" Or, "Can that glass or those mirrors be manufactured without seams?" It was endless but the hours flew by each day for Jack, and he had to say, for the most part, he had never felt so satisfied.

The one point where they almost parted ways was over the theme of the casino resort. Jack felt strongly it should be something futuristic; Vince argued that it had to be something from the past, saying the future would be hard to glamorize, especially the way the world was going. Hordes of designers descended on them. Jack was able to participate in these meetings and the dozens of others through the same closed-circuit television they had employed for the Gaming Commission hearing. They finally decided on a mix of French and Italian designs spanning two or three centuries, in other words, something that never existed in real life in any cohesive way. One designer termed it "baroque," which Jack, on his remote mike, said, "Yeah, baroque, like we're going to go broke if we do it."

"The thing is," Vince broke in, "Vegas is all about imagination! So what if it's not real and never was? That's the whole point." Vince fairly swooned over the drawings for the cocktail waitresses—elaborate high wigs reminiscent of Napoleon's day, but when viewed from behind the servers (men and women) would be wearing nothing more than thong, a velvet one at that. A full-scale, or maybe even larger-than-scale, replica of the Arc de' Triomphe would house an up-scale gentlemen's club. The Leaning Tower of Pisa just off the hotel lobby would contain, what else, a pizza café. All in all, the resort would have eleven restaurants, four swimming pools, one clothing optional, a spa, shopping mall and a casino space equaling three football fields. If the design was a mash-up, just as the financing was, it would still be unlike anything Las Vegas had ever seen. And it would be big.

Chapter Twenty-Seven

Construction on the mega-resort went on for two years, and it spurred other development as well. Comedians began to joke that the high-level construction cranes were Nevada's new state bird. Investors from all over the world poured money into both high-end and outlet shopping malls, as well as new entertainment venues, restaurants and "destinations"—usually boutique hotels surrounded by classy shops and restaurants with lush gardens and pools. Las Vegas was seeing a rebirth, and Jack told Vince one night over their traditional cocktail, "You were the visionary for all of this. I just wish you got more credit for it all." Vince preferred to remain in the background, and he and Jack even agreed to a Board of Directors being put in place to manage their yet unnamed resort.

It had become a game between them. Each morning Jack and Vince would exchange slips of paper with a proposed name. Oftentimes Vince would accuse Jack of drinking too much whiskey the night before, or Jack would tell Vince he needed more coffee that morning. But finally the golden morning arrived and on Vince's 'ballot' was the word Eroe. Jack was puzzled. "You mean like eros, erotica, like that?"

"No, my boy, listen and learn. Eroe is Italian for hero." He paused, "You get it?"

Jack frowned. "Yeah, I get it, but I don't know who else but your Guinea friends will get it," he teased

Vince. "I think everyone else will think what I first thought, you know, not a place you'd bring your family."

"No, no, where's your vision, Jack?" As usual Vince's explosive enthusiasm took over. "I picture the whole lobby being ringed with huge bronze statues of heroes from around the world, you know, uh, uh…" He fumbled, "Like Winston Churchill or Gandhi or, well you know, there's lots of them." He looked more closely at Jack, "And, well, you, of course."

"Oh yeah, any sculpture of me would look like modern art run amok," Jack said sadly. "And before you go any further, no, we're not having one of me in any shape or form." After a moment of thought, however, Jack seemed to warm to the idea. "I like it, I think. Eroe."

Vince snatched a piece of toast off Jack's breakfast tray, chuckling and chewing as he walked out the door. "Buona giornata!"

It had been Jack's idea to build a labyrinth of tunnels beneath the resort and corridors hidden behind the major walls defining any of the public areas, the casinos, showroom, shopping mall and restaurants. His reasoning is that they would function like the tunnels beneath the streets of Chicago or London, allowing freight to be moved more easily without disturbing the guests. It had a side benefit, however, in that it allowed Jack to move through the resort virtually unseen except by security staff who had been told not to approach him. Jack had taken to wearing a cowboy hat tipped low to hide his face, dark glasses and a long-sleeve shirt, although that disguise couldn't hide his hook or his rolling gait dragging his prosthetic leg.

From his suite in the hotel next door Jack was able to see all of the steel framework being put in place for the new resort, as well as the pools being dug and the hundreds of concrete trucks lining up along the side streets waiting to fill the huge pumps. It was endlessly interesting to him and made him wish that he had had a chance to see a carrier ship built as well. The scale was what intrigued him most.

When the buildings themselves were nearly complete, the next phase began of decorating, furnishing and equipping Eroe. One morning Jack looked out to see a string of moving vans perhaps a mile long. As they pulled up to the loading docks it was clear that they all held mattresses—four thousand in all. How many men would it require to assemble all those bed frames, Jack wondered? The next day even more vans delivered bedroom furniture, flat-screen televisions, linens. Even though Jack had seen the budget numbers, it was still staggering to think of the money being poured into the Las Vegas economy before Eroe's doors even opened. In all, the 5,000-room resort would need a staggering fifty tons of linens and 8,000 employees to open its doors to what was projected to be 70,000 visitors a day.

Vince had been astute enough early on to partner with another Las Vegas company, this one specializing in gaming equipment, slots, roulette wheels, craps tables, and the like, so each piece that was loaded onto the casino floor earned Vince a small bonus, a fact he kept hidden from the other partners, including Jack. After all, he deserved a little something extra for all his hard work in putting the idea together in the first place, didn't he? Before any of the gaming equipment could be installed and tested, however, the surveillance gear had to be in place, the famous "eye in the sky" that allowed security to watch every aspect of the gaming operation. Here, too, Jack had some input, insisting that the "eyes" be placed throughout the resort. He sold Vince on the idea by explaining that it might lessen the number of actual security guards needed to watch the mall, the pools and the bars, but even Vince recognized it was just Jack's way of wanting to see everything that went on in the resort without having to mingle with the patrons.

Eventually the older hotel where Jack had been living would be folded into the new resort, and Jack was kept involved in designing a more palatial suite than the one he had enjoyed. He insisted on walls of windows, tinted to block any possible vision into the suite, of course. He also had one separate room designed for the hundreds of cameras to capture the video and audio feeds coming from the surveillance monitors. Vince had suggested he include a small gym in his suite but Jack rebuffed the idea, saying his body no longer held any interest for him, nor would it ever interest anyone else. Vince knew better than to discuss it with him.

Opening night finally arrived and Vince insisted Jack be present. Curving staircases led from the casino floor to Juliette balconies with heavy maroon velvet drapes partially closing them off. Here Jack stood, wearing a mask similar to that of the Broadway actor's in "Phantom of the Opera." The other partners dressed in period costumes as well. Vince donned the costume of Figaro from "The Barber of Seville," complete with orange pantaloons and floppy black hat, bowing grandly to the guests below. Jack carefully kept his hook behind one of the drapes, waving only occasionally with his right hand.

Greg and Bruce were among the throngs of guests on hand for the spectacle—and the free food and endless champagne. Greg wisecracked, "Sort of reminds you of the opening of Pahrump Place, huh?" as he snagged another glass of bubbly.

Bruce could only stare in amazement at the opulent resort, although his mind was whirling with calculations about how many slots and how many tables and what they could be pulling in every minute. "Yeah, it takes money to make money," he agreed with his partner ruefully. "I can't even imagine what they had to come up with to makes this place happen."

"Or what they had to do to get it," Greg muttered under his breath.

Chapter Twenty-Eight

The name Eroe became synonymous with decadence and opulence. One television advertisement featured a sultry-voiced woman barely covered in a length of purple velvet cloth, reclining on a chaise in one of the Eroe rooms asking, "Can we help you escape to a new level of…satisfaction?" Jack rejected another proposed ad that clearly depicted the sounds of a couple having sex and ending with the woman moaning, "Oooh, you're my hero." He told Vince, "We want them down on the casino floor, not up in the hotel rooms screwing." Secretly, Vince thought Jack was just embarrassed by the campaign, and it was modified to show a rakish-looking man winning big at the craps table, a blonde on his arm telling him, "Oooh, you're my hero."

Apparently the ad campaign and word-of-mouth, plus overwhelming media coverage, worked as Eroe was ninety-five percent full every night and would have been one hundred except that the "partners" insisted on always having a few rooms at their disposal.

Every movie and television star yearned to be photographed stepping from one of the resort's signature dove grey limos with their lavender halogen headlights. Vince even had the genius idea of creating a lounge just for the paparazzi so they could monitor the arrival of every limo and every luxury car. The top entertainers in the world brought capacity crowds to the luxurious showroom — no crammed theater seating here, but instead luxury leather recliners with cocktail tables attached to each and cocktail service provided by the most stunning men and women ever to grace the Las Vegas Strip.

One night Eve Gold, whose career had never really recovered from *The Corner Saloon*, pulled up to the valet station by herself, albeit in the most recent model Jaguar. The paparazzi took a glance at her but no one leapt to take a photo. She dropped the car keys into the awaiting valet's hand but declined his offer to unload any baggage. She sashayed into the lobby and went directly to the concierge's desk. "Excuse me," she said imperiously. "I am a close friend of Jack Hamilton, and I would like to be directed to his suite."

If the concierge and half the security people had a dollar for every time a woman made such a request, they could all retire. "No one sees Mr. Hamilton without an invitation," the concierge replied quite firmly. And he could have added, "And no one ever gets an invitation."

"But if you'll just call up and let him know Eve Gold is here," the star insisted, just as firmly.

"I'm afraid I can't do that, miss, what did you say your name was?" The concierge, of course, knew quite well who she was and that her unpleasant reputation preceded her. "If Mr. Hamilton wished to see you, your name would be in our directory, and it most definitely is not." As an extra dig, he couldn't help but add. "Would you like me to validate your parking slip before you leave?" Although few hotel employees had ever met Jack Hamilton, or even seen him, they were nevertheless protective of America's hero.

Bruce and Greg were having drinks in the Pisa bar off the lobby and witnessed Eve's arrival and hasty departure. "I guess he can do better these days," Bruce commented, pointing toward the actress who was clearly leaving in a huff.

"Oh, poor girl," Greg whined. "Why don't I go see if she needs a substitute?" Greg reminded Bruce of the "Pigpen" character in the Peanuts column—habitually with his shirt half untucked, food stains on his tie, and scuffed shoes that had never seen a coat of polish. Bruce, since he was usually calling on doctors and hospital administrators, was just the opposite, always sartorially correct but never too flashy. A custom-made Italian suit might have contrasted with his oh-so-sincere demeanor and spiel about running a simple care home in Pahrump.

Jack watched Eve's arrival and departure many times on the security camera feed, alerted to it by a signal from the concierge. For a moment he thought about allowing Eve to come to his suite, then stepping from the bedroom and asking, "How do you like me now, baby?" Would she play up to him in his deformed state just to see where his connections could take her? He'd accused her once of being a whore and doubted things had changed much. No, he would stay in his luxurious cocoon for the time being. He loved to slide the panel back to the room in his suite that hid all of the surveillance cameras and often spent hours on end sitting there watching. He also enjoyed roaming through the miles of tunnels winding through the bowels of the casino. Even isolated as he was from the reality of the mega resort, he could still feel its palpable energy. Of course, he also had his daily reports from Vince to provide even more "color." The man came up with a funny story or an interesting challenge every day, something Jack looked forward to as the highlight of his day. "So, here's the thing. We know this guy has a hooker on his arm and he's losing big at the tables. Then we hear his wife has decided to fly to Vegas to surprise him and is on the way to the hotel," Vince pantomimed a shocked look. "So, we want to keep him losing big, but we've got to ditch the hooker and pronto." Jack knew Vince would have an ingenious solution, and Vince didn't disappoint. "So, we find this *other* guy, and he's *winning* big, and badda bing, badda boom, we just happen to get her away from the loser and introduce her to the winner. Nothing a whore likes better than money." Vince was laughing to the point of tears and soon Jack was, too. "Oh, and the loser, he sees his wife coming in the door and slips the pit boss a hundred dollar chip to thank him for getting rid of the bimbo. So, everybody's a winner, well, except for the loser, but at least his wife's not going to take him to the cleaners."

Every such night seemed to end pleasantly for both men although Vince hated to see Jack so sequestered in a prison of his own making. Vince was very surprised, therefore, when Jack made a request.

"I think I would like to have a car," Jack asked Vince very seriously. "Or, a truck. Yeah, I think a truck. Nothing fancy, but new, you know?"

"You can have any damn truck in the world," Vince responded immediately. "But, hey, you know our limos are always at your disposal."

"No, I know, but I'd like a truck just the same for when I want to…go somewhere." Vince said he would take care of having one delivered the next day in Jack's favorite color, blue.

Chapter Twenty-Nine

As per usual, Vince popped into Jack's suite at breakfast time, which Jack had taken to having at a leisurely nine or ten in the morning. Vince was bouncing on his toes, obviously eager to tell Jack something, but he waited until Jack pushed his plate away. "Okay, here's the thing. I contacted the Ford, Chevy, GMC and Toyota dealers here in town and asked for their top-of-the-line trucks, in blue, and oh, baby, you should see what's parked down in the garage awaiting your approval!"

Jack yawned, "Well, I'm sure any one of them will be fine," then pulled the newspaper toward him.

Vince nearly exploded until he saw the grin cross Jack's face. "Why you…don't tell me you don't want to run right down there."

Jack faked another yawn. "Oh, if it will make you happy I guess we could head on down." He couldn't help but laugh just looking at Vince. You would have thought the truck was for him! Vince was excited about the trucks, of course, but more about what they represented—that his friend Jack would finally open up to the world apparently. Vince chattered about the truck features all the way down in the private elevator. "Did you know they're almost always automatics now?" And, "The technology. Good thing you're young so you can still learn how to use a Bluetooth, whatever that is."

A section of the underground garage had been emptied of other cars and there sat four gleaming pickup trucks ranging from a robin's egg blue to a deep navy with gold pin striping. Each had custom alloy wheels and were four-wheel drive. The windows were darkly tinted, a necessity for spending any time driving out in the Nevada desert, and Jack observed, a good way to protect his privacy. Jack went first to the Ford and inspected its roomy cab and leather seating. Again he was glad to still have his right arm in order to pull himself up into the trucks. Ultimately he picked the royal blue Chevy with tan leather interior. "Whoo boy, if the guys in Texas could see me now," he almost said aloud.

Vince got on the phone and closed the deal for the truck, then called his assistant to ask her to have the other trucks returned. He almost thought about keeping one for himself but realized how ridiculous a short Italian in a sharkskin suit would look getting out of one of the behemoths. No, I'm strictly a sports car guy, he thought. He handed the truck keys to Jack. "You ready to take it for a spin?"

Jack hesitated but pocketed the keys. "Maybe later. I'm suddenly a little tired. I'm going back up."

Other than moving out of his former suite at the old hotel into his current digs, Vince realized this was the first time Jack had left his suite since coming to Las Vegas more than two years ago. It probably was a bit daunting for him. But it left Vince wondering, where was Jack planning on driving? He hoped there might have been a woman involved that Jack was planning to go visit, but dismissed that idea in a second. It had to be something else.

He was still mulling it over when he visited Jack that evening for their usual cocktail hour and Jack shocked him once again.

"I know there are hundreds of them in town, but can you find a good, reputable — if there is such a thing — tattoo artist and have them come here?" Jack asked.

"A what?" Vince almost choked on his drink.

"You heard me, a tattoo artist, a person who does tattoos," Jack replied, a little annoyed. "I could go through the computer or whatever, but you can ask around." He thought for a minute. "Check out some of the tattoos on our employees and see who has a good one that was done locally."

"You planning to get a screaming eagle on your chest, or what?" Vince teased him. "Or maybe tattoo some eyebrows back on? I hear a lot of women are doing that?" He started to laugh even though he knew Jack was getting angry. "Now that you've got that fancy truck, are you starting to think about drawing attention to yourself, too?"

"I am not and it's none of your business," Jack snapped. "I'm sorry I asked you. I'll handle it." With that, he went into his surveillance room and slammed the hidden panel shut, leaving Vince holding his drink and wondering what had gotten into his partner. "Christ, next he'll be wanting me to find him a psychic." He finished his drink and wandered down to the casino floor to begin looking at tattoos, knowing Jack was doing the same thing through the various eyes in the sky.

It was Vince who could have used the services of a psychic, however, as the next day's events would prove.

Chapter Thirty

Vince had found Jack a competent tattoo artist who agreed to work in Jack's suite for as long as it took to complete whatever design Jack had in mind. The pony-tailed, heavily-inked man of about forty arrived promptly at ten the next morning and was shown by security up to the fiftieth floor. Jack had a massage table set up in the living room with clean sheets and whatever else he thought a tattooist would need.

"Bill Dempsey, pleased to meet you," the man said, extending his hand to Jack while taking in his overall appearance. "War injury? Iraq?"

"No, West Texas oil field, but that's not why you're here," Jack said amiably. He'd left orders not to be disturbed, even by Vince. "I have something else in mind." He pointed to a piece of paper on the massage table and asked, "Think you can do that for me?"

Dempsey looked a little surprised but shrugged, "Yeah, sure, no problem. You don't want a little art or something to go with it? I'm great with flames," he said expectantly.

Jack actually laughed. "Nope, had all the flames I ever need to see."

"Okay, then, get comfortable," Dempsey said, motioning to the table and setting up his supplies.

"I'm going to clean the area first and then I'll put a little local anesthetic down."

"The burn areas really don't have much sensation, but okay." Jack was a little surprised at the first touch of the needle but settled down quickly. He was pleased that Dempsey didn't seem to want to make small talk as he worked.

Some four hours later, Dempsey leaned back, stretched and rubbed a bit of an alcohol cleaner over his work. "Well, there you go." He chuckled, "Of course you'll be reading it backwards in the mirror, but trust me, it's all spelled right."

And there it was:

Do Not Resuscitate
Do Not Intubate
Do Not Medicate
Do Not Notify Anyone

The type was black with a thin red outline and it was centered directly over Jack's heart. Dempsey had taken the liberty of putting a border around the words in the design of lightning strikes. The whole thing was about five by five inches. Jack had a thousand dollars in cash waiting which he counted out while Dempsey applied a light bandage. "Don't submerse it for a few days but you can shower." He further cautioned, "There will be some sloughing of skin, but if you see any redness or sign of infection, call me, man." He took the money and shook Jack's hand again, pleased to see that Jack seemed more than satisfied with his handiwork.

That evening when Vince stopped in, he immediately asked, "So, do I get to see this new work of art?"

"No. You don't, and I hope you never do see it," Jack added mysteriously, pouring Vince his customary Scotch. Vince seemed to drop the subject without even teasing Jack, surprisingly, and Jack noted he seemed worried.

"So here's the thing," Vince began, settling into a wing chair holding his glass in both hands. "I got a visit today from some of the partners." He blew out a huge breath. "They want to bring in some of their boys from Atlantic City and make a few, uh, adjustments."

Jack looked at him quizzically. "In what?"

"Well, for starters, the slots. They think maybe they're not paying off enough."

"What the hell? We've got billboards all over town and halfway to Los Angeles saying ours are the loosest in town!"

"No, Jack, paying off enough for *them*."

The two men's silence said it all. Vince shuddered at the recollection of how one of the partners suggested Vince talk to his "very close friends" at the slot machine company. Did they know about his secret side deal?

Vince made himself a rare second drink. "And there are certain *procedures* they want changed in the counting room."

"They can't change anything in the counting room. The Gaming Commission would be on our ass so fast we wouldn't know what hit us," Jack protested. "They know damn well that room is under constant video surveillance and recording."

"Well, here's the thing," Vince began sadly. "They say they've been able to fix that in Atlantic City and the commission there never caught on. They say they're taking an extra million dollars a day out of there."

"So, it's a skim, am I right?" Jack said, the color rising to his face. Vince nodded and hung his head. "Those bastards are making millions legitimately but it's still not enough?" He slammed his drink down on the table, spilling half of it. "We're not doing it. That's all there is to it. We're honest men and the fact that we got in bed with some snakes is…regrettable, but we can't let it ruin us." He took a deep breath. "And it's my name, and my name only, on the gaming license. If they threaten us, I can shut this damn place down."

"Whoa, whoa, Jack. Come on. It's not going to come to that."

"So, what are you proposing? We just bend over?" Jack's anger was building but Vince tried to remain at least outwardly calm.

"I think we look at it as just another cost of doing business, like payin' off the union," Vince said seriously. "We let them make a few adjustments, nothing too big, and then…"

"Then they'll want a few more 'adjustments,' as you call them." Jack was pacing by now. "I don't know how you can tell me this so calm and matter-of-fact like."

"Jack, they've got some, umm, motivational tools," Vince answered sadly. "My family, for one."

Vince had never talked about his family although Jack assumed it was the typical large Italian clan. "They've threatened your family! Let me get this straight. *Our* so-called partners have threatened *your* family!" Vince nodded his head and Jack had to restrain himself from throwing his cocktail glass across the room.

After a moment he sat down on the sofa across from Vince. "Do they know about that 'poison pill' provision you had the lawyers put in my contract when we got the license in my name?"

Vince brightened. "No way. It's you, me and the lawyers." He actually clapped his hands together. "You want to tell them, or you want me to?"

"Oh, no, the pleasure will be all mine." He stood and walked toward the windows. "Nobody else takes advantage of Jack Hamilton." Vince joined him taking in the view of The Strip at night. The two clinked glasses. This could work out after all.

Chapter Thirty-One

Jack had taken to leaving Eroe in the hours before dawn in his new pickup, heading straight for I-15 and out into the Mojave Desert. He turned off on every paved road he came to and explored for a few miles, or sometimes a few hours. He knew what he was looking for and was sure it was out here. Still, he managed to be back in the resort in time for breakfast and in time to beat the punishing heat, which even through the tinted windows tormented his burned skin.

The second or third time he left the hotel on one of these outings, security contacted Vince. "Do you want we should follow him?" the guard asked. "Or, we could GPS his truck, you know?"

Vince was amused but said, "No, he's a grown man, well past thirty, and if he wants to go out for a drive on his own, just let him." Vince could just imagine Jack going into orbit if he thought someone was tracking him. Vince, for his part, was just pleased that Jack was going anywhere and doubted it was anything dangerous. Ironically, the current danger was *in* the hotel from the partners in town to discuss the hotel's "adjustments."

Jack had called a closed-circuit meeting with the partners for noon that day, news Vince delivered personally to each one and was met with the same protests. "He's too good to show his face to us? He wants to sit up in that tower and dictate to us?" And on, and on. Vince tried graciously to explain to them about Jack's disfigurement and his severe anxiety concerning his appearance, but they were not buying it. In truth, they were correct at least on one level.

Jack told Vince bluntly. "I'll never sit down at a table with those pigs, or maybe I should say I'll never pull up to a trough with them." Despite their reluctance, the East Coast partners piled into one of Eroe's conference rooms at noon, pleased at least to see a sumptuous buffet lunch with dozens of bottles of wine already open.

Jack opened the meeting. "Gentlemen," and he thought to himself, I use the term loosely. He was, of course, hidden by a screen but watching the conference room from several different angles on closed-circuit. "Vince Ciriglio has informed me of the changes you want to make to our operation here. I want to stress to you that this is *our* operation, Vince's and mine. Every idea you see in Eroe is something *we* have developed."

At this point one of the partners interjected, "Yeah, and we paid for it!" The other partners grumbled in assent, but Jack reigned them back in.

"You wouldn't know whether to shit or go blind if you had to run this place for even an hour! I don't care how much money you've got in it." He paused. "You have all gotten your initial investment back ten times over. You show me any other business in this economy that's doing even half as well." He could see several of the dozen or so partners talking with each other.

"Let me also remind you of a provision of my contract, the contract that allowed this casino to open its doors in the first place," Jack said, waiting for the men to stop talking. "I am the sole, the only, the one name on the gaming license, and furthermore I am President for life of AHG." He saw one of the men make a sign like a gun with his thumb and index finger. "Let me also tell you about another provision of my contract which you…gentlemen…overlooked in your haste to get your fingers in the pie." He paused until he was certain he had their full attention. "If anything happens to me other than death by natural causes, this entire resort, casino, hotel, every goddamn inch of it, goes to the Arch Dioceses of the Catholic Church of Southern Nevada."

There was a sharp intake of breath all around the conference table and several men tugged to loosen their ties. One pounded on the table. "You can't do that! What the hell would the Catholic Church do with a casino?"

"I don't care if they make it the world's largest, most luxurious homeless shelter and soup kitchen," Jack said evenly, enjoying their distress at learning about this "poison pill." Almost in unison the men reached for the wine bottles to fill their glasses.

"The point is this," Jack said, pulling aside the screen so he could look at them with his one remaining eye.

"At least Vince and I are honest and we are not making any adjustments to our operation that are illegal in any way. If you can't accept it and want out, we can buy you out this afternoon—in cash." The partners were shocked and confused, which is just what Jack intended. "That offer stays on the table for one hour, during which you can enjoy your lunch—on the house, of course." Waiters moved in to uncover the warming trays, and Jack could almost smell the lasagna and veal chops himself. "I'll be at the casino cage in one hour for anyone who wants out." The partners were in a virtual stampede for the food, but Jack had one other thing to make clear before he switched off the television monitor. "And don't think that you can threaten me with anything. I've already lost everything a man can lose and I'm still standing."

But that's where Jack was wrong. He did have something to lose and it was Vince. His mentor, partner and friend was found shot to death in the casino garage that night in what the Las Vegas police described as a "gangland-style hit." A follow-up story in the Review Journal described Ciriglio as the "brains" behind the development of Eroe. Instead of making Jack angry, it made him proud because it was true.

Chapter Thirty-Two

If anyone thought Vince's death would make Jack back away from gambling and from Eroe, they were dead wrong. Jack threw himself into it with a vengeance because that's what he was feeling. He brought a management team in to run Eroe on a day-to-day basis although he still watched the surveillance feeds every night, especially from the counting room. He also sent out feelers to every other casino: Were they interested in selling? Was there property on The Strip that begged for development? He had no interest in Atlantic City, riverboats with gambling operations, or in Indian casinos. Las Vegas was his only concern, and defeating the East Coast mobsters who thought they could muscle in just because they had money when Jack and Vince had needed it. Well, he didn't need it anymore. Privately, he grieved Vince's loss, especially at the end of the day when he realized he had truly no one to talk with. But, he mused, maybe it made life easier in the long run. His anonymity might be his strength. The Las Vegas media had long ago closed ranks to protect him, never attempting to steal a photograph of him. He occasionally gave telephone interviews and he was always described as "reclusive" and "thought to be suffering from the disfiguring effects of a Texas oil field fire."

Over the next eighteen months Jack, through the AHG, acquired four more properties, three casinos and one hotel, and plans were put in place to expand some and consolidate the others. The Gaming

Commission offered no opposition since Eroe had run a very clean operation with no cause for concern. They accepted the explanation that Vince's slaying was related to events years in the past in New Jersey and had nothing to do with his activities in Las Vegas. Jack did make sure that certain members of the New Jersey Gaming Commission heard the whole story, including the mobsters' ways of conducting the skim in Atlantic City casinos without their knowledge.

Jack also set up a dummy corporation with the goal of buying out each of the investors that had conspired to murder Vince. He wanted to be rid of them once and for all, even if he paid a premium to do it. The acquisitions of the new properties was costly but they were well-chosen and the profits allowed Jack and his board to eliminate the original investors entirely. They could go back to Atlantic City or they could go to hell; it meant nothing either way to Jack.

Bruce, on the other hand, would have been happy for even one of Jack's investors. He and Greg had acquired a few more trailers for Pahrump Place and built a stucco wall around the whole compound, making it look like an adobe-style building, more attractive for the web site they had also put together. Greg had been in favor of simply finding an existing adobe building in another state and photo-shopping it into the web site and brochures. Any corner was a corner to be cut as far as Greg saw things. It was one of the reasons the unlikely partnership worked; each had a certain streak of larceny.

One morning Greg bounded into Bruce's office on a rare occasion when Bruce had decided to visit the Pahrump facility and dropped a thick medical chart on his desk. "We've got a winner! Winner, winner, chicken dinner. Wait till you see this!"

Bruce flipped the chart open and glanced at the intake form. Clara Willis, age 83, transferred from Sunrise Memorial Hospital, no family, no religious affiliation, last address Desert Palms Assisted Living. Diagnoses: Multiple strokes, aphasia, congestive heart failure, and the catch-all, failure to thrive. Bruce looked up, "So?"

"The *so*, my man, is on the next page." He waited expectantly until Bruce broke out in a grin. "So?"

The old lady had been widowed for nearly thirty years, drawing her husband's full railroad pension for all that time plus her own retirement as a teacher. She must never have spent a penny of any of it, Bruce observed, since she had amassed nearly a million dollars in a money market account. She also had untouched brokerage accounts and more than a hundred thousand dollars in a checking account from which she had paid her rent at the upscale assisted living facility. "Well, the poor dear," Bruce said, sounding like the wolf stalking Little Red Riding Hood. "Get the paperwork started and get your butt over to the lawyer's office pronto."

Greg grabbed the chart off Bruce's desk. "You know, I'm thinking maybe we need a little commission structure. Call it a finder's fee." Bruce's grin was replaced by a frown, so Greg didn't pursue the issue, at least not now. "I'm on it. She'll be all ours within a day or so. Of course, in the meantime we'll take such good care of her." Both men laughed out loud. Poor Clara would be lucky to last out the week.

On the other side of the Spring Mountains Jack was just returning from one of his early morning drives out into the desert. Now that the casinos and hotels were finally on an even keel, he had resumed his prior practice of heading for the Mojave. The desert had a calming effect, and away from the light pollution of Las Vegas he was able to enjoy a sky full of stars, something he remembered from his days out in the ocean on the destroyer. His search in the desert had been conducted in ever widening circles, but Jack knew he'd eventually find what he was looking for, and finally he did.

The building was rusting in places and the hangar door hung at a precarious angle. The runway had potholes big enough for a man to lie down in. The runway sock was shredded years ago. A fuel pump off to the side held a rotting hose and had clearly been dry for years. Tumbleweeds had built up on one side of the hangar in places six feet deep. The glass was broken out of all of the windows and it looked like many people had used it for target practice. In short, it was perfect.

Despite his undeniable success in the gaming industry, Jack still felt that he wanted to create something that was entirely his own. He had contributed ideas and strategies here and there to Eroe and the other properties, but he still viewed that as Vince's success and not his own. In his heart, Jack saw himself as a designer and builder, and if his oil well venture had failed, there was nothing to say that his next idea wouldn't be a complete success. He could feel it in his bones, but still, he wasn't willing to pursue his idea in public just yet. He used his truck's GPS to get an exact reading of where the abandoned hangar was located. When he returned to the hotel he would find out who owned it and, through one of his shell companies, buy it by nightfall.

Chapter Thirty-Three

Over the next several months Jack further extricated himself from the day-to-day operations of the casinos, although he still reviewed a profit statement every week and marveled at just how fast the money poured in; he was rich beyond his wildest dreams. But he was also bored and lonely. He would occasionally see something on the surveillance cameras that he would just have to remember to tell Vince about later, but then it would come back to him. There was no Vince to tell, and no one else either. Finally, Jack realized he had to make plans to move on his next project. He had easily acquired the abandoned airstrip and hangar out in the Mojave but then never drove back to even look at it again.

After the notorious July monsoon season had more or less ended, Jack thought he should go see if the place had washed away in the flash flooding common in the desert during the brief but torrential rains. He left Eroe at his usual four in the morning and was at what he referred to as 'the site' an hour and a half later. The rains had carried away many of the tumbleweeds, he noted, so there actually had been some improvement. He was terrified of snakes, probably the only thing he was afraid of, but set out to explore the inside of the hangar, a large stick in hand.

Sturdy steel racks lined both sides of the building which Jack estimated to be about four thousand square feet, large enough for two small planes and an office space which still contained a beat-up desk and chair. A closet held a small bathroom with a shower, sink and toilet, although everything needed to be replaced before Jack would even consider setting foot back in it. He wished he'd brought a tape measure and a notebook, but as he sat on the edge of the desk he could see his dream taking shape.

Bruce's dreams were taking shape, too. When he and Greg, through Pahrump Place, LLC, had "inherited" Clara Willis' estate, Bruce had initially thought of acquiring another facility, but this time in Las Vegas, sparing him the odious task of ever visiting Pahrump again. Greg, the slob, had come to be as happy in Pahrump as anywhere else and said it was easier to meet women in the casino there because they weren't so particular. The more Bruce thought about it, the more he realized that as much as he hated making the sixty-mile drive to Pahrump, the state nursing home regulators probably dreaded it too, and the more distance he was able to keep from them the better. Lea's family had moved there in droves, not only working for Pahrump Place, but also opening the town's first nail salon, a laundromat and two convenience stores. Bruce rarely saw Lea except when he visited the emergency room where she still worked. He did notice that she had an engagement ring twinkling on her hand, and he felt somewhat relieved about that.

So, they decided to sit on the money for a while and maybe start looking at the little one-horse towns scattered north along Highway 95. Greg said he knew of at least two whore houses that had shut down near Beatty and might make ideal care centers. They had suspected the facility in Pahrump might have been just such an establishment, and their suspicions were confirmed early on when men arrived at the door looking to see the "girls." Greg howled with laughter every time he thought of the looks on the men's faces when they saw the eighty- and ninety-year-old women lined up in their walkers.

Pahrump was about a hundred miles, as the crow flies, from Jack's site, but the atmosphere could not have been more different. Jack began making daily trips out to the hangar, although he had still not told anyone what he was doing. The security staff at Eroe dutifully washed his pickup every afternoon when he returned it, noticing more dust and debris in the bed with every trip. One of the more enterprising staff finally ordered a bed-liner for the truck to protect its brilliant blue metal-flake paint job, and another guy installed mud flaps, none of which Jack even noticed.

"Maybe he thinks he's not rich enough, and he goes out prospecting for some lost gold mine," one of the guards joked after cleaning the truck.

"Well, he's not trolling for chicks with all the crap he throws on the floor of the truck, that's for sure," another joined in. "I think he just goes out to howl at the moon, or maybe he found some magic hot springs that he can soak in." The men just shook their heads and each thought it was sad that America's hero was reduced to such a poor existence.

But Jack was in his glory. Every day he made lists of supplies and materials he needed, and he had begun doing the hard physical work of cleaning up the site. He hadn't realized how out of shape he had become just sitting in his hotel suite. He had found sun-resistant long-sleeved shirts and pants, as well as a hat with a long flap to cover his neck and found those made it tolerable to work out in the sun, and with fall approaching, it was much cooler, too. His hours of rolling a ball around or putting pegs into holes in physical therapy paid off as he could do most chores quite handily with his hook, a realization that pleased him to no end.

He did notice that quite often when he took the exit off I-15 that eventually led to the series of dirt roads leading to the air field that there was the same young man just sitting by the exit, not attempting to hitchhike, just sitting, leaning up against a road sign. One day Jack's curiosity got the best of him and he pulled up next to the kid and rolled his window down just an inch or two. "Do you need a ride?"

"Nope."

"So, somebody comes here and picks you up every day?"

"Nope."

Jack surveyed the vast expanse of empty desert and felt stupid for even asking. "Do you work somewhere around here?"

"Nope." The kid finally stood up and approached Jack's truck, but not too close, and Jack's window wasn't down far enough for him to see inside. "But I see you every day. Do *you* work around here?" he asked.

Jack couldn't tell if he was mocking him or not, but he decided to answer anyway. "Yes, I do. Or, I will." The lanky young man said nothing. "I bought that old airstrip seven or eight miles from here and I'm fixing it up."

"Oh." And then after a long pause. "Yeah, I know the place. My old man used to deliver fuel out there."

"Oh," Jack said, not knowing where else to take the conversation. "So, you know it needs a bit of fixing up."

"Yep. I guess it would."

The conversation died just as a gust of wind blew up a dust devil not far from the truck. Jack decided to make a bold move. "Uh, I have to tell you, there's something...wrong with me."

"Oh, they's all kind of folks out here with something wrong with 'em," the kid, who looked to be about eighteen or twenty, said slowly. "That's why they're out here, all to hell and gone."

Jack rolled down the truck window, giving the boy a full look at his scarred face with its empty eye socket and putting his hook out the window, dangling it alongside the door.

"Cool." The boy didn't seem to even glance at Jack's face but he was clearly fascinated by the hook. "Can you make it do stuff?"

Jack demonstrated how he could click it together and rotate it a bit. "I've only got one leg, too."

"Does it have a hook?"

"No, it's just like a leg, with a foot and all," Jack replied, thinking it was the strangest conversation he had ever had. "Do you live near here?"

"Oh, a ways back, but I come out here to think," the young man replied seriously. "Sometimes somebody stops, but not usually."

"Well, I'll stop and say hello, at least," Jack ventured, "unless you'd prefer I just drive on by."

"Nope. That'd be all right I guess."

"Okay, then. I'll be seeing you, probably tomorrow." Jack rolled the window up and the kid gave him a slight nod. He rolled it back down. "My name is Jack. You?"

"Henry Cash, but mostly people call me Hank on account of my dad is Henry, or was Henry."

Jack felt awkward just leaving him there by the roadside. "You want I should give you a lift?" The kid shook his head and went back to sit by the road sign. Jack pulled away slowly so as not to kick up any more dust, but as he looked in his rearview mirror he had the thought that Hank was just what he needed.

Chapter Thirty-Four

The day after their first chance meeting out in the desert, Jack did return and was pleased to see Hank sitting by the side of the road again. "Get in. I've got a job for you," Jack yelled out the window.

Hank, it turns out, was twenty-one and had graduated from high school in Barstow, another Mojave Desert town that was basically a refueling stop for travelers between Los Angeles and Las Vegas on the original Route 66. He had no brothers or sisters and his mother moved away to "somewhere in Texas, I think," when his father died. Hank's father drove a fuel truck servicing air fields and small, non-chain gas stations. One night on the desolate stretch of I-15 between Barstow and Baker, a drunk driver lost control of his car and crossed the meridian, hitting the fuel truck head-on. The drunk driver died instantly but Hank's father survived with burns over seventy percent of his body. "They'd operate on him every few days and try to get the dead skin off," Hank explained, "but in the end he was beggin' them to let him die." He finally did, which went a long way toward explaining why Hank showed no particular reaction at seeing Jack's burns. Hank lived on a small Social Security benefit in a single-wide mobile home in a park that had largely been abandoned. He got free space rent in exchange for fixing whatever broke. "I'm good with my hands, I guess," he told Jack one day. "I can just find stuff and make things." Jack could relate to that.

Of course, all this information had to be dragged out bit by bit over the course of nearly six weeks of working side by side nearly every day. Their working together, however, seemed the most natural thing after only their first day together. Hank's taciturn nature fit in well with Jack's plans to keep his project under wraps. Hank asked nothing about Jack, and Jack didn't know whether Hank realized who he was or not, or if the young man simply didn't care.

Vince had started the tradition of leaving a thousand dollars in cash in an envelope in Jack's desk every day, but since Jack never left the hotel in those days he had amassed quite a bit of cash. So, at the end of every work day he handed Hank a hundred dollar bill. He always waited for Hank to ask for more, but he never did. Every morning when Jack pulled up to the road sign to pick Hank up, it seemed that their relationship had to start from scratch, and finally Jack realized it was because Hank didn't trust Jack to return or trust himself to hope that Jack would.

Jack was forced to trust Hank, however. "Can you drive?" he asked his new employee.

"Sure."

"Okay, then, here's a list of things I need from Home Depot. I guess the one in Barstow's closest," Jack said, handing Hank the list of building supplies and the keys to the truck, plus an envelope of money. If Hank didn't come back, Jack thought, he'd have a long walk home through the desert. But Hank was back at the hangar in about four hours and mutely handed Jack the keys before beginning to unload the tools and supplies.

"Oh, I used eight dollars to get us some sandwiches," he said shyly. "I can pay you for mine, though." He handed Jack a sack.

Jack just laughed. "Good thinking. Not too many restaurants in this neighborhood, after all." He'd ask the casino staff to pack them a lunch from now on, and he added a refrigerator to the list for the next trip to town.

Hank surprised Jack at the end of one of their work days. The hangar had been thoroughly cleaned and repaired and was bulging with tool chests, outfitted with a metal lathe, table saw and huge work tables, although one area slightly bigger than Jack's truck was kept pristinely clean. "So," Hank began. "You planning to buy a plane, smuggle drugs or something?" He saw Jack's shocked expression. "I mean, don't mean nothin' to me, lots of people do it out here. Good money and all." He thought about the wad of hundred dollar bills Jack always had at the ready.

Jack knew it was a lot to get two sentences in a row out of Hank, and he didn't want to embarrass the young man who up to this point had simply done any chore Jack assigned him. "No, nothing like that," he replied carefully. "Everything's on the up and up and always will be." He motioned Hank to sit next to him on the truck tailgate. "You say you're good with building stuff, and I can see that you are. But now you're going to have a chance to really build something you can be proud of." He put his hand out as if to shake hands with Hank. "If you'll be my partner in this we're going to build the most exciting new private airplane the world has ever seen, and we're going to fly it off that strip right out there."

"Do you fly?" Hank asked, incredulous at Jack's revelation.

"Nope. You?"

"Nope." The two burst into laughter.

"I guess we'll learn then!"

By now the refrigerator had been delivered and Jack pulled two beers out, using his hook to open the bottles, something that made Hank chuckle every time.

Chapter Thirty-Five

Jack had drawn crude plans for the plane but realized he needed the advice of an expert aeronautics engineer. He was still obsessed with the "power of the prop," as he called it, and the plane would feature two rear-mounted propellers, pushing, instead of pulling, the plane forward. He found an engineer in Los Angeles that would be willing to look over the plans, and in a few weeks Jack got his answer in a call from the man, who had himself designed several experimental craft.

"It's ingenious but risky," the engineer told Jack. The two talked for nearly an hour with the engineer suggesting what sorts of weight-bearing changes needed to be made and how the angles of the wings should be adjusted. He promised to draw his changes and send Jack a detailed schematic by the end of the month. In the meantime, he told Jack, there was work he could start on and Jack made a list. He hated to be idle for even a day, in sharp contrast to the years he spent just sitting in his hotel suite watching the surveillance feeds. He could tell Hank was anxious to get going too.

When he received the detailed schematic drawings accompanied by a binder full of notes, he sent the engineer a money order far greater than what the man had originally asked, and he sent him something else. The nondisclosure agreement meant that the engineer could never discuss this consultation or the design of the plane with anyone. The penalties would be severe in monetary damages and perhaps even lead to the revocation of the engineer's licenses. Jack wanted to be certain if this plane were a failure, news of it would never see the light of day. After seeing the substantial payment, the engineer signed the multi-page legal document and returned it to Jack the next day; he never did know who his secretive client was, as Jack had conducted the entire transaction through another dummy corporation.

Jack spread the plans and the notes out on the large work table and suggested to Hank that they go through them step by step to see what they were capable of doing themselves and what might have to be contracted out. The process took days and although both men thought they were able to build just about anything, they finally agreed on sending the fiberglass fabrication out to a specialist as well as the on-board fire suppression unit and dozens of small pieces that would take them more time to create than they were worth. The motors and controls they felt confident of building themselves, as well as the framework for the body and the wings.

Hank was on the road half the time between the hangar, Barstow and sometimes as far as the Los Angeles Basin, rounding up the parts they needed based on Jack's meticulous lists. One night as they were having a beer and double-checking everything Hank had unloaded that day, Hank told Jack, "I may be late tomorrow, but not too. I'll call you when I get to the sign post." Jack had gotten cell phones for both of them which made communications much easier when Hank was on one of his supply runs.

"Oh, what's up?"

"Well, it's my mom," Hank began. "She likes to uh, call me on my birthday."

"I didn't know you were still in touch," Jack asked.

"We're not, except for this, I guess." It didn't appear that Hank was about to say any more about the subject, so Jack let it drop.

"Okay, so call me." Then Jack had a second thought. "You know I've got some things in Vegas that need tending. What do you say we both just take a day off?"

Hank drained his beer and nodded his agreement. Jack would have a busy day ahead.

Jack vividly remembered how excited he was (and how much he tried to hide it) when Vince presented him with a lineup of shiny new pickup trucks, and he thought it would be fun to do the same for Hank. Although he spent very little time at Eroe, he still had an administrative assistant to handle the myriad of details and issues that arose every day. He called him as soon as he got back to the resort that night. "I need you to get me full-size, crew-cab, 4 x 4 pickups, fully loaded, and they have to be red. Get one from each of the brands, you know, Ford, Chevy, Dodge, and so on." The assistant made notes and wondered what Jack had in mind. "Then get ahold of a car carrier service that can pick each one up tomorrow—doesn't matter if they need two or three carriers." Now he ran into a problem. He didn't want to tell his assistant where he spent his days, but how could he tell her where to deliver the trucks? "Get started on that. I'll call you again in a half-hour or so."

He mixed himself a drink and thought again about Vince and how smoothly he had handled everything. Jack had never considered the stress Vince must have experienced. Here a simple thing like buying a truck had him flummoxed. He called his assistant again. "Okay, one more thing. Get a red Corvette to go with the trucks." They talked about the 'Vette for a few minutes. "Tell the car carrier service to call me on my cell phone once they're fully loaded, and I'll give them directions. I want them picked up tomorrow. You confirm with them that they got all the trucks. Then they can plan to deliver them the following morning." Problem solved. The assistant was intrigued and a little bit excited to go truck-shopping; it was certainly more interesting than dealing with one of the resort's restaurateurs agonizing over changing the color of the dinner napkins.

Jack could barely sleep that night. It had been so long since he'd done anything personal for anyone, and it felt good. He hoped Hank would be half as excited as he was. He forced himself to stay busy with resort details the next day, but the following day he was up before dawn, loading lunch and a birthday cake into his truck.

Hank looked a little dejected when Jack met him at the road sign a few miles from the hangar. "So, did you have a good talk with your mom?"

"Nope."

"She didn't call?"

"Oh, she called all right."

Jack realized he'd have to pry the story out, as always. "And, she's okay?"

"Okay? I guess so. She's getting married."

"Wow, that must have been a surprise," Jack agreed.

"Yeah, on account of she's gonna have a baby."

Jack was nearly as stunned as Hank and scrambled for a reply. "So, you're going to be a big brother then."

"I ain't gonna be nothin' to that kid or to that whore of a mother." Hank looked like he might actually cry as he ground his fist into the palm of his other hand. "Dad barely a year in the grave…"

They drove the rest of the way in silence with Jack wondering if he should turn the truck carriers around.

Chapter Thirty-Six

Jack called the carriers and asked them to wait until noon for the delivery. "No problem, it's your nickel," the lead driver told Jack, swearing to himself about having to sit out in the Mojave Desert for a few more hours. Jack put Hank to work right away, figuring he'd gotten all the conversation he was going to get from him for a while. Jack even wondered, what if his own dad had died first and mom remarried? Would he care? Of course, with a baby it was a different deal entirely.

Hank was welding some struts for the wheels when Jack called the carrier and gave him explicit directions to find the remote air strip. He told them to pull in and unload as quickly as possible, placing the trucks and the Corvette in a horseshoe formation. "No problem, boss," was the surly reply he received. There goes your tip, asshole, Jack thought.

The trucks were quite a sight against the dull California desert backdrop. Two were fire-engine-red, one more of a burgundy, and two definitely candy-apple red. The Corvette was a deep burgundy with candy-apple red rocker panels and deeply-tinted rose windows. Jack carefully placed the birthday cake on the hood of the 'Vette and stood back to admire the tableau. He couldn't help smiling broadly and anticipating Hank's reaction.

He went back into the hangar and tapped Hank on the shoulder. "Hey, you've got to come outside. I didn't know you ordered all this shit." Hank looked bewildered but turned off the welding torch and took off the bulky welding helmet. He followed Jack out of the hangar.

"I didn't..." Hank started to say, then saw the array of vehicles. He stood stock-still with his hands hanging at his sides until Jack lit the candles on the birthday cake. "What the...?"

Jack was practically bobbing up and down with excitement and waited for some reaction from Hank. Maybe Hank was playing the same game with him that he had played with Vince? But no, Hank turned away and walked rapidly back into the hangar, donning his welding helmet and firing up the torch. Jack blew out the candles on the cake and signaled the carrier drivers to stay put.

"Hey, buddy, it's your birthday, man," Jack said, approaching Hank, grabbing him by his left arm so as not to disrupt his welding with his right arm.

Hank stopped welding and turned angrily toward Jack. "If you think all this, this..." and he threw out an arm encompassing the hangar, "is to get me to be like your boyfriend or something, well, go to hell."

Jack couldn't help himself. "You're too damn ugly and stubborn and silent and humorless and," and by this time he was laughing so hard he couldn't continue. "You're not my boyfriend and you're never going to be, you jerk. You're my friend and my partner, and it's your birthday." Hank was beet-red, whether from the welding helmet or his statement was impossible to say. "Get your ass back out there and let's celebrate!"

Hank walked back out to the landing strip and this time his eyes did light up as they roamed from one truck to the next, flitting back to the Corvette between each one.

"So pick one and let these guys get back to Vegas," Jack told the birthday boy. "I can't have you putting any more miles on my truck." He elbowed Hank in the ribs. "Red is your favorite color isn't it…sweetheart?"

Hank walked from one truck to the next, opening the doors, peering in the truck beds, admiring the wheels. "Well, we've already got a truck for business stuff," he started. "I'm thinkin' maybe someday we'll have to go someplace fast and…"

So it was going to be the Corvette, just as Jack had sensed. Hank was a young man, after all, and a new red 'Vette would have a lot of currency with the young ladies of Barstow.

Jack gave the 'round-em-up' signal to the carriers who winched each truck back up onto the transporters, one of whom flipped the keys to the Corvette to Jack. He caught them handily with his hook, embarrassing and astonishing the driver, but provoking a laugh from Hank, as always.

On the other side of the range, Bruce was watching a car carrier do his job, too. The Mercedes he and Greg had felt would be a valuable asset to their image was making its way slowly up the ramp. The money good old Clara had left them was being rapidly depleted and a luxury auto just wasn't in the picture. Greg didn't care since he never got to drive it anyway. Bruce kept pushing and pushing and pushing him to find more 'poor souls' like Clara and at the same time cut every expense possible at Pahrump Place. It was getting damn tiring and if they hadn't been friends since business school, Greg would think about moving on. Every time he brought it up, however, Bruce would reassure him about the big money yet to come. Truth be told, Greg was too lazy to go out and look for anything else unless it fell from the sky right into his lap.

Chapter Thirty-Seven

Jack gave Hank a couple of days off to enjoy his new Corvette; he half expected Hank to actually sleep in it. Jack used the time to meticulously inspect all of his lists to see that they had every part they would need to begin assembling the plane. The fiberglass pieces had come in a week earlier, and both Jack and Hank were in awe of how spectacular they looked in a red, white and blue design. For the time being the cabin itself would be sparse, only two seats and a storage area, but the seats were leather and matched the fiberglass design.

When Hank returned from his little vacation, he was a changed young man. He was smiling for a change and radiating a new confidence. He hugged Jack as soon as he saw him, something he had never done in the past. "Hey, man! I had so much fun!" Hank said with enthusiasm. "When I drove by our road sign this morning, I thought, no more sittin' out in the dirt waitin' for nothing." It amazed Jack that a car could make so much difference in Hank's attitude, but a little later in the morning Hank actually explained the change. "I don't think I've ever had anything new in my life," he said solemnly. "The church always gave my folks toys or a bike or something for me," and he plucked at his shirt, "and most of my clothes. When I got older, I could wear my dad's worn-out shirts." He scowled. "By that time the church had pretty much given up on us anyway." He had parked the Corvette where he could see it out the front door of the hangar. "That car says that I am worth something and I have places to go in my life."

"I'm pleased I could make it happen for you, Hank." In truth, Jack was embarrassed because he'd pretty much always had whatever he wanted. "When we get this plane built, I think the place you have to go is college." Hank snorted. "No, I'm serious. There are technical schools where you could really learn a valuable skill. You're so smart." Jack tossed him a wrench which Hank caught without even looking. "And, good with your hands."

From that day on the mood lightened considerably in the hangar, and it was a good thing because building the little plane proved much harder than either of them anticipated. Jack understood the times when Hank jumped in the sports car and roared off in a cloud of dust; it was his way of dealing with the frustration. For his part, Jack just made more lists, and lists of the lists.

One relationship that was not being improved, however, was that between Bruce and Greg, and it was largely due to frustration in their operations as well. "I'm telling you, they're dying like flies," Greg complained one morning. "We can't keep the beds full with people who are just going to die."

"Well, duh, they're in a nursing home because they *are* going to die," Bruce snapped back, shaking his head. "We just have to get a better class of patients."

"Yeah, and we're going to do that in Pahrump!" Greg slammed his hand on Bruce's desk. "You said you'd get in with the docs in Summerlin and Henderson, the high-end areas, and they'd just rush to fill our beds." He pointed his finger at Bruce. "You might be getting in with the nurses there, but you haven't produced shit. I doubt there's a doctor in either of those hospitals who even knows who you are!"

Bruce sat stone-faced and just let Greg vent. "Perhaps you would like to go to Summerlin?" he sneered at Greg. "You'd make such a sterling impression with your ratty clothes and your eight-dollar haircut."

They'd had the same argument many times before and this one ended the same way the others had. "I'm just frustrated that we've put almost five years into this and all we have is a collection of crappy trailers in the middle of a crappy town," Greg allowed. "And I have to live here while you're off in Vegas doing who knows what."

"I can't spend time out here and be recruiting patients in Las Vegas," Bruce said patiently. "You know that." He felt a little bit sorry for his former classmate but had no intention of spending any more time in Pahrump than he had to. The desert held no appeal for Bruce.

It still had a great deal of appeal for Jack who was happy to sit on the tailgate of his truck at the end of the day and watch the sun set over the mountain peaks, casting long shadows across the desert. The

Joshua trees looked like people, he imagined, and reflected about what the early pioneers must have thought when they first encountered this challenging landscape. Early on, he had brought a Gulfstream travel trailer out to the hangar site and spent many nights there, enjoying the quiet punctuated only by an occasional coyote yip.

After just such a night Jack awoke refreshed and was able to clearly see the engineering problem that had baffled Hank and himself. He made a pot of coffee and waited for his young partner to slide into the parking lot. The plane's schematics were spread out on the work table, and Jack had already highlighted in red the changes they would have to make. Hank arrived bearing doughnuts and went straight to the table. Within seconds, Jack could see that he had grasped the solution as well. The coffee and doughnuts were soon forgotten as Hank fired up the welding torch and Jack unscrewed the fiberglass panels. That day was the most satisfying of any they had put in. The plane would be air-worthy in just a couple days, they were now certain.

"Don't we have to get those numbers, you know, I don't know, from the FAA? To put on the tail?" Hank asked suddenly.

Jack knew what he was referring to but decided to deliberately lie. "No, we don't get the identification numbers until we can prove the plane actually flies. Then we'll get 'em." Hank seemed to accept the deception and no more was said about the subject.

Jack believed and hoped the plane would fly, but if it didn't, he wanted to be able to dispose of it without anyone being the wiser.

Chapter Thirty-Eight

Hank's mother called again, but this time it was from a hospital in a Dallas suburb. Her new husband had beaten her to the point of a miscarriage, plus broken her nose, an orbital rim and several ribs, and dislocated several of her fingers. Before the beating, he had also thrown all of her belongings out into the front yard; no doubt they had all been stolen by the time she woke up in the emergency department.

"Hank, honey?" she cried softly into the phone. "You gotta help me. I got no one here." Her plea was met with the stony silence she had expected, but she had to try. "Won't you help your old mom get back home at least, and then I won't bother you no more, I swear."

Hank swore under his breath. "I'll send you a bus ticket." His mother started crying even louder. Since she had called on Hank's cell phone, Jack was in the hangar to hear at least Hank's side of the conversation. "I don't know what the hell you saw in that loser in the first place," Hank said angrily. "And then to think you'd have a baby with him!" Jack signaled him to tell his mother he'd call her right back, which Hank did.

"All right, it's none of my business..."

"You got that right," Hank snapped. "Stupid bitch. Asshole beat the hell out of her, she lost the baby and now I'm supposed to get her out of Texas."

"Well, that's bad business for sure," Jack started again. He knew Hank's mother was all he had left. "A man that'd hit a pregnant woman is no more than a worthless coward." Hank stood sullenly, flexing his fists. "But, she is your mom and all both of you got, really." He hastened to add, "I mean, you've got me, but it's not the same as the woman who gave birth to you."

Hank turned on his heel and headed out of the hangar toward his car. Jack heard the motor come to life and knew Hank would burn rubber halfway down the airstrip. He was surprised, therefore, when he heard the motor shut down just as suddenly. He fiddled with some parts on the work table and tried to act busy, waiting for the frustrated young man to come back inside. "Okay, I called her back and I guess I'll have to drive out there and get her and all her crap, or what's left of it."

"That's fine," Jack said almost too quickly. "And you should take my truck instead of the 'Vette." He tried to gauge Hank's reaction. "Can't be haulin' crap in that car." Hank seemed to consider the offer.

"Yeah, but you need the truck to get those parts," pointing to one of Jack's ever-present lists.

"Oh, I can always get hold of another truck," and he laughed. "Don't worry, I won't be haulin' greasy parts in that baby of yours."

They spent a few minutes discussing what else needed to be done to the plane and concluded it was mostly cosmetic or comfort-related, no heavy mechanical work. Jack had found a simulator in Los Angeles that would take the plane and "virtually" fly it as a test, and the plan had been for he and Hank to get it loaded on a semi then follow it to LA.

"I sure wanted to see that simulator flight," Hank said wistfully.

"I know you did, but here's the deal." Jack himself had no plans to reveal himself to the operators of the simulator and had already arranged with them to film the "flight" and make a copy available to him. "I'm going to get a film of the whole deal and I'll have them send one right to your phone at the same time. Wouldn't that be cool? We'd still be watching it together, in a way."

Hank broke out in a half-smile. "Okay, partner, I guess we would, huh?" They agreed that Hank would stay at the hangar two more days to help get the plane loaded up for its trip to the LA basin, then he'd leave at the same time for Texas, figuring on a two-, maybe three-day drive to Dallas. Jack insisted on arranging for a hotel for Hank's mom in the meantime.

The semi arrived early in the morning and backed carefully up to the hangar. "If that isn't the damnedst-looking thing I ever did see," the truck driver exclaimed on seeing the plane with its rear-mounted props. "It don't know whether it's comin' or goin'." He noticed the frowns on both of his customer's faces. "But, hey, that's some beautiful fiberglass design." The semi had an attached forklift that easily slid under the plane's fuselage and lifted it toward the open doors of the truck. The wings had already been detached and were crated separately, with detailed instructions to the staff of the simulator about how to reattach them.

"I still wish we were going down there with it, especially to put the wings back on right," Hank said, looking like a parent about to send his child off to kindergarten for the first day. "I mean, what if..."

Jack clapped him on the shoulder. "They'll get it right. That's why we designed it the way we did, remember? So any pilot can pick it up, pack it up, and put it away if they want, even in their garage." Hank seemed a little bit reassured but still looked on nervously as the truck driver adjusted the cargo straps and climbed down from the trailer. He gave Jack a copy of the bill of lading and climbed into the cab, giving the air horn a little tweak as he pulled away, heading for I-15.

When it came time for Hank to actually leave for Texas, Jack pressed a handful of hundred dollar bills into his hand. "I know, I know, don't start with me about how you don't need it." Hank already had his mouth open to protest but instead gave Jack an uncharacteristic hug and turned quickly away, waving just a little as he stepped into Jack's truck, dreading the dull drive to Texas and the drama that awaited him. Jack felt numb, watching the two things he cared about the most drive away into the desert.

Chapter Thirty-Nine

It would fly! Jack and Hank watched their creation lift easily off the ground in the simulator, wind flowing beneath and above the wings in the exact proportion necessary. The simulator operator banked it from side to side without a hitch, and raised and lowered the nose of the plane smoothly. The videographer hired by Jack even became excited by how successful the first flight was. "Look at that!" he could be heard saying in the background. "It just floats right along." It landed just as easily.

When the filming was over and the plane removed from the simulator, the company president himself came on the line to Jack, although by now Hank had disconnected. "I say, Mr. uh?"

Jack hesitated, "Cash, Henry Cash."

"Mr. Cash, you have got a real winner here. I've seen a lot of planes come through here, and I'm a pilot myself, but I tell you, this is going to be big." He was so enthusiastic. "I'd buy one myself. Anyone who wants to be a casual, weekend-type pilot will love this, just love it."

On the other end of the line, Jack wanted to let out a good old Texas "Yee haw!" but restrained himself. "Well, thank you sir, I'm so pleased to hear that." He thought about Hank out in Dallas. "We've put our heart and soul into this project." He thought for a second. "I guess we have to come up with a name for our little craft here."

"Oh, that's easy," the president said. "Call it the Flying Cow, as in Cash Cow, because that's what it'll be!"

"Somehow a flying cow doesn't really conjure up the right image," Jack laughed heartily. "We'll think of something, I'm sure. Thank you again." He disconnected the conversation and sat in the hangar deep in thought until the sun had long since set. He didn't know why he had switched identities with Hank on the spur of the moment, but the more he thought about it, the more he knew it was the right thing. He had always wanted to do something that was "just his," but ironically now he had given it away. If anything happened to him, at least Hank would have the plane and all the rights to it. They never had written a formal partnership agreement, and Jack knew that if the legal team at Eroe had gotten wind of the project, they would have been all over it, writing every clause possible to exclude Hank, not include him, but Jack would remedy that situation tomorrow, instructing them just how to draft the partnership. If the simulator president were correct, someday Hank would be a rich man, just as Jack was already. The thought of it made Jack genuinely happy.

Greg and Bruce were already awash in lawyers, and it was not making them happy. Bruce had been dating a woman in Pahrump who had some sort of federal job in Las Vegas, but of course, he didn't pay any attention to what that job might be. To him, Carla was just a local convenience for the times when he was stuck in Pahrump overnight. Her door always seemed to be open and she seemed grateful for whatever little attention he provided. But then one night Lea came to Pahrump to see her family, and Bruce decided it would be a nice gesture to at least take her out for a steak dinner at the local Nugget casino. Lea was bubbly about the plans for her upcoming wedding, and Bruce had to admit she looked positively radiant.

Carla thought so too, when she saw the couple, heads close together, sitting in a booth in the steakhouse. She had always known she was the jealous type, and seeing Bruce with another woman sent her into a rage (even though she had to admit they didn't have anything close to a relationship). Should she confront him? She didn't have the nerve, but she had something better—information.

Bruce had bragged endlessly about how adept he had become at scamming the feds with his nursing home operation, getting job-training grants when no training was provided, energy assistance funds, and so on, all to make himself look like a bigshot. Now Carla was just sure that the federal prosecutor in the office next door to hers would love hearing all about it. "Enjoy your steak, asshole," she thought with a smug satisfaction. "Your next meal might be on a prison tray."

Sure enough, Carla was correct, and within weeks Bruce and Greg found themselves sitting across from an assistant federal prosecutor with a stack of files a foot deep on his desk, all files from Pahrump Place. "I will admit," Bruce said obsequiously, "we did have some, um, tenuous accounting practices, which I'm sure I can explain."

"I think it's a lot more serious than tenuous accounting practices," the young attorney replied. "We have evidence of you accepting more than five hundred thousand dollars in grants and fees and providing not one hour of documented training." He pulled out a notepad. "And that's just in the three programs you've enrolled in that I've had time to review." He rocked back in his chair. "These are very serious charges, and I urge you to take them so."

"Oh, we do, certainly, sir, we do," Greg stammered although Bruce seemed to be in a staring contest with the prosecutor. "I think if we could just…"

"I *think*," Bruce countered, leaning forward, "that you will have to give us solid evidence of your findings and that in the meantime, we will go back to running a legitimate business that provides a much-needed service to people no one else cares for." He seemed almost pious. "I hate to think what would happen to these valued elders without us."

"I think," the prosecutor replied scathingly, "that you are unprepared for private enterprise and you think ripping off the federal government is somehow justified in the name of, what did you call them, 'valued elders' when in actuality, those people are being preyed upon by you and your partner here." He gathered the folders together. "I'd advise you to get your ducks in a row because we're not dropping this matter. Now, if you'll excuse me." He picked up everything and left the two partners in the conference room.

Greg looked nearly ill, but Bruce just shrugged. "Stupid feds. It'll take him a year just to find his own ass with both hands. In the meantime, Greggy-Boy, we just keep on keepin' on." He sauntered out of the room as if he was leaving a cocktail lounge.

Chapter Forty

Jack heard the semi truck's air brakes release out on the airstrip and walked out to greet the driver. Now it was Jack's turn to feel like a worried parent, this time that his child got home safely. The driver made the usual complaints about I-15 traffic while he undid the doors and lowered the ramp on which the forklift sat. He positioned the forks precisely and slid the plane out, swiveling the forklift and setting the plane gently on the pavement, then put the forklift back on the ramp and drove it into the truck to retrieve the wings. Jack stood by anxiously but the whole operation took less than ten minutes and Jack could see the driver was a professional. He had to remember to call Hank and tell him their little eagle was back in its nest.

"Do you have another load to pick up this afternoon?"

The driver took his gloves off and closed up the back of the truck. "No, I'm done for the day, dead-head back to Vegas and wait for a load there."

Jack reached for his ever-present roll of hundreds, prudently turning his back so the driver didn't notice, and peeled off two. "I wonder if you could help me," and he raised his hook, "just take an hour or so, to put the wings back on? It's a two-man job." He held up the hundred dollar bills.

"Not a problem," he readily agreed. "Always happy to help a fellow veteran. You're a veteran aren't you?" he asked, looking at Jack's disfigurement and guessing at his age.

"Oh, you can definitely believe that," Jack sighed. "Persian Gulf."

The driver nodded knowingly. "Afghanistan, two tours." He grabbed a crow bar and began unpacking the first wing. "Don't talk about it much though."

"Works for me." Jack pulled the packing material away from the wing as the driver splintered the wooden case. The fiberglass wings were perfectly intact. They did the same with the second crate. The wings were lightweight and Hank had already fabricated a stand that they could rest on at the right height to attach to the plane. They had the wings reattached in no time.

"Look, I'm sorry I said what I did about this plane," the driver began. "But, the guys down in LA said it did okay, huh?"

"It sure did." Jack, eager to show anyone, pulled out his cell phone and cued up the video for the driver to watch.

"Well, look at that, just smooth as silk, all right." He shook Jack's hand. "Job well done. I'm happy to have helped you out." Jack gave him an extra hundred and the driver clambered back into the truck, giving Jack a final wave as he drove off toward Las Vegas.

Jack walked back into the hangar and heard his computer printer start to churn out sheets. It was the contract he had asked the Eroe attorneys to draw up giving Hank eighty percent of the as-yet-unnamed aircraft company. In the event of Jack's death, his own twenty percent share would go to the Wounded Warriors project, Jack had decided. The contract looked straightforward and Jack signed it right then, leaving it on the work table. He'd probably wait until Hank came back to talk to him about it, and he knew the young man would want to refuse.

He looked at the plane sitting on the tarmac, just sparkling in its red, white and blue fiberglass with just a hint of metal-flake. Damn it, why didn't he ask the truck driver to help him get it in the hangar! And why wasn't Hank back yet! He saw his own frustration and laughed at himself. Maybe I should jump into Hank's 'Vette and go work it all out. Hank probably noted the odometer reading before he left! Oh well.

Jack climbed up into the plane's cockpit and marveled at how snug and comfortable it was, the instrument panel a picture of efficiency. They had splurged on the leather seats and on the carbon fiber for the panel, in a faux walnut design, but it all came together perfectly.

What was not coming together perfectly was Hank's efforts to get his mother loaded into the truck and headed for California. Even though her louse of a husband-to-be had beaten her half to death, she still cried on Hank's shoulder that she loved the bum and she was sure he would change. Hank looked around for the TV cameras, thinking it was the perfect daytime soap opera. Jack had graciously paid for a hotel room for Hank's mother until Hank could get her and her few remaining possessions packed up to leave Texas, and Hank felt he couldn't impose on Jack's hospitality one more day. "You've got until eight o'clock tomorrow morning to be outside that hotel, waiting for me to pick you up," he told his sniveling mother. "If not, I'm going back to Barstow and you can do what you like." He jumped into Jack's truck and shot out of the parking lot. Damn it, why wasn't he back in the desert helping Jack!

But Jack had decided, maybe he didn't need Hank's help this one time. He started up the motors and felt the props kick into action. He'd seen Hank do the same many times to drive the plane into the hangar. How hard could it be? First he had to taxi out the runway and turn the plane around. He'd have to remember to talk to Hank about putting in a reverse gear. He remembered he'd forgotten to call him to tell him the plane was back.

The little plane taxied out just as smooth as could be, Jack felt, and when he reached the end of the runway, he just felt like a kid again and wanted to do it one more time, so he drove back toward the hangar.

Then, rather than driving it in, he turned around again. He thought about the plane in the simulator, lifting so smoothly as more power was applied. He set off down the runway, gently increasing the pressure on the gas pedal, hearing the props whining a little more loudly, and then he felt the plane's wheels leave the ground.

Chapter Forty-One

At about the time of Jack's lift-off Hank was walking through the house his mother had shared with the jerk, trying to salvage what little was left of her belongings. After he had beaten her up, he'd tossed most of her things out into the yard, and those were long gone. But Hank saw a few pieces of furniture that might be worth taking and most of the kitchen stuff. He doubted she'd be waiting outside the hotel in the morning, but he had to do what he could. The jerk, as he regularly referred to him, refusing even to say his name, was still in jail so Hank had no fears about running into him at least. He made a pile in the living room of the things he'd load into the truck in the morning. Even though the couch was pretty ratty looking, Hank decided he might as well just sleep there for the night and see what the morning would bring.

In the morning Hank showered and shaved at the house, then loaded the truck within a few minutes. There was a Starbucks down the street, and although he ordinarily wouldn't have spent that much money on a cup of coffee, today he felt he deserved it. He fumbled through the multitude of choices, aware that cars were piling up behind him in the drive-through, finally receiving a small cup of rich black coffee hot enough to scald a lobster. He held it gingerly with the tips of his fingers and drove slowly to the hotel, aware that he would be more than a half-hour early.

She was sitting on a bench outside the hotel, suitcase beside her, smoking a cigarette. Her dark glasses hid the black eyes, but it was obvious she had been through some trauma just from the careful way she held herself. Hank jumped out of the truck to grab her suitcase, tossing it in the back. She took a cursory look in the truck bed, noting what he'd packed but said nothing to Hank; he said nothing in reply and they pulled out into the traffic, heading ultimately for I-40 and at least two long days of driving.

Hank's mom, Julie Ann, looked out at the barren landscape of Texas and thought, "Hell, I might as well be in Barstow."

Hank watched the miles roll by and thought, "Hell, I wish I was in Barstow."

They finally began to talk when they saw the "Welcome to New Mexico" sign. "So, I guess Texas is officially behind me," she started.

"I hope to hell it is," Hank said, sounding harsher than he planned. He was sure she was uncomfortable sitting for hours, and he hadn't allowed much time for rest stops along the way, generally at fast-food restaurants where they could use the restrooms and get back on the road in minutes. He watched his mother look blankly out at the desert, hearing her sigh occasionally.

"I don't think I really want to go back to Barstow," she said. "People will just look at me like I'm some kind of loser, which I am, I guess." She was a woman in her early forties who looked much older, owing to years living in the dry high desert of the Mojave with very little in the way of luxuries. Her mousy brown hair had never been much and now there were patches where the jerk had yanked it out by its roots. Her skin was sallow from the hospital stay.

"You're not a loser," Hank tried. "You just 'made bad choices' like they say on TV."

"Well, I had my dreams, and dreams are darn hard to give up," Julie Ann sighed, starting to tear up. Hank noticed and looked straight ahead.

The day before and a thousand miles away, Jack had the same thought about his dreams. Maybe he wasn't quite ready to let go of his. He felt the plane's wheels lift off and knew he should have backed off, but instead he pulled the wheel back and felt the plane rise steadily, leaving the airstrip behind and soaring out over the flat desert. Jack felt a moment of the most intense, pure joy he had ever imagined. He was free from everything on earth in this dazzling creation that was all his own. He thought about what Hank would think and remembered again that he had to call him.

He practiced banking the plane slightly in each direction with the foot pedals, and it was so responsive, even with his prosthetic leg. Jack smiled broadly. "I could stay up here forever." That sentiment lead to a more sobering thought, however. Eventually, the plane would have to land. He thought of Hank again and how they had laughed about whether either of them could fly a plane. "We'll learn!" they had both guffawed. "We'll learn." Well, Jack thought, I guess one of us will anyway.

Just then a strong thermal current the desert is famous for knocked Jack out of his reverie, jolting the plane sharply upward. Jack hit his head and was dazed for a moment, then the plane hit another thermal, and without thinking, Jack pulled back on the wheel, sending the plane into a steep climb. By the time Jack realized what he'd done, it was too late. The plane was in a stall and being buffeted by the thermals. Jack felt the engines die and the plane begin a slow roll backwards, end over end, throwing him out of his seat and back into the cargo area where he bounced from side to side as the plane continued to plummet to the desert floor. At one point he could see a rock outcropping and knew the crash was imminent. There was nothing to do but ride the doomed craft down.

The lightweight fiberglass plane hit with a stronger impact than Jack would have expected and it was enough to splinter the plane into a hundred pieces, throwing Jack violently out into the rocks. His last thought before losing consciousness was ironic: At least the on-board fire suppression system worked beautifully so he wouldn't suffer any burns.

Chapter Forty-Two

When Jack regained consciousness it was near dusk. In the back of his mind he noted which direction the sun was setting and guessed he was at least fifty miles from the hangar. But, he was far more preoccupied by his injuries as he began to inventory them. Each breath alerted him to a number of broken ribs. His right arm was intact, although his wrist had a knot forming on it. He had no idea where his prosthetic leg was, it having been torn off on impact. His right ankle was bent at an unusual degree and he howled with pain on trying to move it. His left arm and shoulder seemed okay and that prosthetic was still attached. His back hurt where a sharp rock was sticking into him, but he could sit and flex, so that was reassuring. He dragged himself, inch by inch, off the rocks to a sandier resting place and drew an arrow in the sand pointing to the setting sun, after which he slipped out of consciousness again.

He came to at night with a blanket of stars overhead. Although he was in pain, he was still able to appreciate the beauty of the night sky without any interfering light pollution. There was no moon, and Jack didn't trust himself to drag himself much further in the dark since he wanted to be sure to stay to a westward direction. "There's another thing I should have paid more attention to," he thought grimly, "astronomy. I would have known which direction was west." He fell back to sleep, to be awakened by the sun scorching down on his bare head. He looked at the arrow he had drawn yesterday and began dragging himself along until the sun on his burnt skin, combined with his other injuries, forced him back into unconsciousness.

The next vision he had was of Eve Gold, beautiful in a diaphanous blue gown, her auburn hair down in waves over her shoulders. She was slightly turned away from him, but when she felt him looking, she swiveled to face him. The sneer she produced was pure Eve. He imagined that he tried to reach out for her, but she just laughed in her haughty way and pulled back. "Oh, you're such a star, maybe a falling star this time." She slipped away, laughing under her breath.

When Jack fully came to again, he realized she had been a dream, or a nightmare, more like it, and that he was still trapped out in the unforgiving Mojave, slowly roasting. He had to find some cover and some water. He pulled himself along doggedly, thinking perhaps he should have stayed with the wreckage; there might have been some protection from the sun there at least. But no, if he was going to die, he didn't want it to be anywhere near his plane. People would think the was the failure when, in fact, it was all on him.

He made a few hundred yards' progress until pain and exhaustion overtook him and he passed out again, this time to be visited by another hallucination. The bodies of the men he had killed in the oil field explosion were lined up in front of him, their families right behind. "But look how it ruined *my* life!" he wanted to tell them but couldn't. Would death have been better than the life he'd had since? Fortunately, his mother was there to cradle his head in her lap. "It's all right honey. It wasn't your fault." Always his supporter.

Mercifully, the sun began to dip toward the horizon, temporarily ending at least part of Jack's agony. He lay on his back, exhausted from his struggles and too dehydrated to even lick the sand from his lips. Jack thought with a pang of sadness about all the useless trivia Hank used to pepper him with about the desert and wished he had paid more attention to that, too. The presence of certain white-flowering plants was a sure indicator of water, he did recall, and began to look about him more intently. This would be the time of year for them to flower, he realized, and believed he saw one about a hundred feet away. Or was that a hallucination as well?

He began crawling again, each bump of his broken ankle shooting pain all the way up his leg and each reach forward producing a grinding sensation in his ribs. By nightfall he had reached the plant, and indeed there were water droplets in the cups of the flowers. His tongue was thick and leathery but he tried to capture every drop he could, then plastered the flowers over his head in an attempt to soothe the burning skin there. He passed out with his face deep in the plant, his arms wrapped around it. That night there were no dreams. In the morning the plant was again full of dew, and Jack thought he might have a chance at survival after all.

He awoke to the sound of his drill sergeant screaming at him, "You're a Marine now! Buck up and act like one!" Jack recognized it as being a figment of his imagination, but he thought it might be just the message he needed. He rested for a while and thought about the kind of soldier he might have been. All the 'kill' had gone out of him as he'd gotten older, but he imagined he would have been as gung-ho as any of the young men who willingly charged into dark houses and rounded corners into alleyways not knowing what might be waiting.

Jack continued his westward path, seeing more of the white-flowered plants as he went along and considering them a good sign. He thought of Hank. He was glad he'd left the signed contract on the table giving Hank control of the plane's future, but at the same time he wondered what Hank would think. Would he think I just took the plane and deserted him, Jack wondered? He supposed somebody would find the plane's wreckage eventually, but without the FAA registration or any identifying numbers, it was likely nothing would ever come of it.

Reluctantly leaving one of the white plants behind, Jack resumed his crawl in the midday sun, cresting a small berm and then, before he could stop himself, tumbling over it, rolling several times before coming to rest at the side of a freshly-graded dirt road. He sobbed in pain and in relief. If the road was in this good shape, someone would eventually drive down it. Before they did, he had one last task ahead of him.

He used his elbows to pull himself back to the berm and began digging a hole. When it was done, he undid the straps on his prosthetic arm and placed it in the hole, reluctantly covering it with dirt and rocks. The state-of-the-art prosthetic was simply too unique and would therefore be easily traceable. If there were a time when Jack treasured his anonymity, this would be it. The oil field fire had successfully burned off his fingerprints, and of course, he had the explicit instructions tattooed on his chest. All he had to do now was wait.

He sensed the sharks circling him and beginning to tear chunks of his flesh away, bumping him back and forth. Then he heard, "Do you think he's dead? See if you can roll him over."

Arms reached under his broken ribs and rolled him onto his back. He opened his eyes to see an elderly man and his wife staring down at him. "His eyes are open, Darla. I think he's alive." His wife looked pessimistic.

"I don't think we should get involved in this, E.J. We don't know what he's doing out here."

"Well, we can't just leave him," the man said doubtfully.

"Oh, if we came along, someone else will," the woman named Darla answered. "Let's get back to our rock-hounding. We haven't been able to get out for weeks."

Jack groaned and with herculean effort managed to reach into the pocket of his jeans, extracting a hundred dollar bill, which he weakly held in the air. "Well, now, he knows we're here, we've got to help him," the old man said, while Darla plucked the bill out of Jack's hand. "Help me load him in the back of the Jeep." Jack lost consciousness again with their jostling, and when he awoke next it was in a trauma bay, the old couple long gone.

Chapter Forty-Three

"Can you tell me your name, sir?" a male voice asked Jack, shaking him lightly by the shoulder. "Sir?" He turned away and spoke to someone else. "He's not saying anything, but I think he hears us." He tried again, "Sir, do you know where you are? Can you tell us your name?" Someone pulled his eyelid up and shined a bright light in his eye. "Okay, get him up to CT. Let's see if there's a bleed." Jack felt the gurney being pulled out of the room and wheeled down a hallway. He kept his eye closed, thinking all hospitals look about the same anyway. When he arrived at the CT scanner, orderlies roughly transferred him from the gurney to the gantry to slide him into the machine. Jack almost told them to be more careful but didn't. He recognized the sensation of being on morphine and for the moment was content to drift along in its haze.

Jack didn't know how long the scan took or what else had transpired but awoke again back in the emergency department. "There's no bleed and no overt signs of trauma," a man, presumably his doctor, said to someone else. "I think he's good to go to the OR and get that ankle fixed."

"What do you think happened to him?" another disembodied voice inquired. "He looks like he's been through hell and back."

"Some of the injuries, the ankle and the ribs, are new, but he was through hell years back, I would say, especially from the burns." Jack sensed the two men move closer to him. "Look at his eye socket. That happened at least ten years ago, maybe more, same with his arm. You can tell there was a prosthesis there at some point."

"Wow, I can't even imagine what he looked like before," the other man said. "He sure looks like Frankenstein's ugly cousin now."

"Being out in the desert for a few days didn't help him any, that's for sure, probably made the scar tissue from the burns even worse." Jack felt the man tap a pen on the gurney railing. "Yeah, poor bastard's had a tough time of it."

"Did you hear about the roll of cash he was carrying? Almost twenty grand in hundred dollar bills." The other man was moving away from the gurney. "I'd say he was a drug runner, got caught sideways in a deal and they dumped him out there to die." He seemed to think for a moment. "Don't know why they wouldn't have taken the cash though."

"Hey, before you go. Look at this," the first man said, peeling back Jack's hospital gown to reveal his chest. "I've never seen anyone with a tattoo like this."

The other man let out a low whistle. "You think that would hold up in court?" They both laughed.

"Not my problem, buddy. I just fix 'em up and pass 'em along to the next guy." Shortly thereafter Jack was passed along to the orthopedics department where a surgeon made no attempt to talk to him although did enjoy some gallows humor with his staff, noting there was no need to mark which ankle they were to be operating on later that night.

They fixed his ankle and the next morning a nurse came into his room to demonstrate the use of an incentive spirometer, something Jack was already well familiar with. "This is going to help you keep your lungs well-inflated," she intoned in a sing-song. "We don't want you getting pneumonia just because those broken ribs hurt when you take a deep breath." She smiled, "Now can you show me that you can do this?" Jack complied, although it did hurt like hell.

He still hadn't spoken a word to anyone and had decided not to for the time being. He could have called Hank, of course, but he was too ashamed. He knew he should never have flown the plane himself, and he didn't think he could face the look on Hank's face when he told him the plane was in a thousand pieces somewhere out in the desert. Pride, Jack thought. It not only 'goeth before a fall,' but also before a movie disaster, an oil rig explosion and now a plane crash. But Jack realized he was still too proud to admit what happened quite yet.

The hospital treated his obvious injuries but they weren't ready to release him on his own because they still weren't quite sure of the whole picture, especially after four days of him not having spoken a word to anyone. Finally the case manager came to his room with the hospitalist doctor assigned to him. "We can't keep him in acute care any longer. He has to go to a step-down unit of some sort." The doctor voiced his agreement, and each of them made notes on their laptops about what he would require.

"Basically, I think he wants to be buried alive," the doctor said ruefully. "I think that's why he's not cooperating."

"You may be right," the case manager said. "In that case, let's make arrangements for him to be sent to Pahrump Place." She sighed. "If this guy wants to be buried alive, that's the place for him." She went off to make the arrangements but the doctor stayed behind, hoping Jack would make some comment, but Jack simply closed his eye and turned away.

Chapter Forty-Four

Hank's mother's mood seemed to lift a little at the sight of the Las Vegas skyline. They hadn't talked much during the drive, but now she asked Hank to pull over at the next exit. "Listen, honey, I think I'm going to have you drop me here in Vegas. I just can't go back to Barstow."

If Hank was surprised, he didn't show it. "Okay, how are you going to live here? Furthermore, where are you going to live?"

"I'll just stay in an inexpensive hotel for a while, get my bearings," Julie Ann said determinedly. "I can always get a job working in one of the hotels, be a maid or something." During their trip she had revealed to Hank that she had a little money put aside and that the State of Texas would be sending her a check from their victim's restitution program, too.

Hank just shook his head and headed for The Strip. "I guess there's plenty of cheap hotels here, all right." They seemed to be clustered a few blocks off the main thoroughfare, and it didn't take long to find several advertising rooms for rent by the week. Julie Ann pointed to one that had a swimming pool, and Jack pulled into the lane for registration, noting with disgust two women who had to be prostitutes loitering outside the lobby. "You best be careful around here," he told his mother as he reached into the truck bed for her suitcase. "You call me tonight, tell me what your room number is and the phone number." He bent to give her a quick hug.

"Aren't you sweet?" She hugged Hank. "Thank you for helping me. I know it was hard for you, and I know you want to get back to work on that airplane project." She started to cry but stopped herself. "You're just doin' so well and I'm so proud of you." Hank thought he might cry but he let her go and climbed back into the truck, watching her until she was in the lobby. He could just make it out to the hangar by sunset and catch up with Jack.

Traffic was light and he pulled onto the tarmac a little before six o'clock. He was surprised to see the hangar doors open but no plane inside, and his beloved Corvette was parked by the Gulfstream. If Jack was there, where was the plane, Hank wondered. He beeped the horn to let Jack know he'd arrived, but Jack didn't come out to greet him as he usually did. He walked into the hangar but Jack wasn't inside, so he went next door to the Gulfstream, but it was empty as well. Hank grabbed a beer and headed back to the hangar.

He set his beer down on the work table and noticed a sheaf of legal papers. He couldn't believe what he was reading and by the time he got to Jack's signature on the last page he was dumbfounded. Did Jack hire a pilot and take the plane someplace? But why would he have left the hangar open like this? Why would he give Hank the lion's share of a company they would form to build the plane? Why didn't he ever talk about this part of the plan? Hank settled in to wait for Jack, feeling like a dog chasing its tail, asking the same questions of himself over and over. When night fell he locked up the hangar and went to the Gulfstream, thinking he'd stretch out on the couch and at least get a nap before Jack came back.

Hank awoke with the sunrise and realized Jack hadn't returned to the Gulfstream. He pulled the curtain back and saw both the truck and the Corvette still parked outside. Now he was getting worried. What if someone came out here and kidnapped him? Or robbed him, Jack always carrying all that money around. They might have robbed him and dumped him out in the desert somewhere. He could be dead. Hank's mind was racing. He'd already made a dozen calls to Jack's cell phone but they always went straight to the message option. He realized he hadn't heard from his mother either, but that's just like her, of course. Damn it, he was so frustrated! Why didn't he ever ask him where he lived in Las Vegas? He finally decided the only thing to do was to get busy working, cleaning up the hangar and making plans to build another plane.

A week went by with no sign of Jack. Hank's feelings vacillated between anger, grief, and frustration, seemingly about every five minutes. Did Jack use Hank's absence as an excuse to just leave him? He couldn't imagine that, but Jack was always so private. Maybe he had a 'real' son somewhere else and a family. Maybe he was hurt somewhere. Maybe he was dead. Hank didn't want to believe it, but somehow that's what his gut instinct told him.

He thought back to the last conversation they'd had, right after the simulator flight. Maybe the guy in charge of the simulator would know where Jack went. Hank called the company and told the receptionist that he and his partner had tested a plane there not long ago and could he talk to the man in charge? The company president came on the line immediately. "Mr. Cash, it's good to hear from you again."

Again? Hank thought, he's never talked to me. "Uh, I was wondering if maybe you've been talking to my partner, Jack Hamilton?"

"No, can't say as I've ever spoken to him."

Hank was stumped.

"Say, Mr. Cash, did you ever come up with a name for that plane of yours?"

"A name? Well, no, not yet."

"Well, you and your partner better put your heads together on that. Let me know when you're ready to start building some more of those beauties. I might like to get in on it, Mr. Cash."

"Uh, yes, I will, sir. Thanks for talking to me." Hank ended the conversation more confused than ever. Where was the plane?

To add to his frustration, his mother picked that moment to call. "I'm not in Vegas anymore," she started.

"If you went back to that jerk in Texas," Hank began, instantly angry.

"No, nothing like that. I got a job and a place to live out in Pahrump," Julie Ann said, indignant at Hank's presumption.

"What the hell's in Pahrump?" Hank didn't think he'd ever even driven through the town, although he knew it as the gateway to Death Valley.

"I'm working at a nursing home, and the fellas that own it provide housing for us, too. I always did like taking care of people."

Hank simmered down. "Well, I guess that's great for you, mom. Maybe I'll drive over and see you one of these days." He never had talked much to his mother but felt the urge to tell her about Jack. "My partner's gone missin' and he left all this legal paperwork giving me the plane company, and, oh, I just don't know what the hell's up."

Julie Ann was surprised at all the information and didn't know quite how to react. "Oh, you'll figure it out, I'm sure. He probably just took a vacation to celebrate or something." Her shift was about to start so she hurriedly gave Hank her new phone and address and said she'd look forward to seeing him real soon.

Jack on a vacation? Somehow Hank couldn't imagine that.

Chapter Forty-Five

Bruce had been correct in his prediction that the federal prosecutor would forget all about Pahrump Place. The fraud he and Greg perpetrated was small potatoes in comparison to the scandal that blew up in Las Vegas. A sitting federal judge was accused of accepting bribes—from a notorious brothel-owner, no less. The newspaper headlines became more lurid every day, suggesting that money wasn't all the judge had accepted. And all of this came at a very bad time for Nevada politics.

Nevada's governor was eyeing a run for the Presidency and vowed to "clean up Nevada at all costs." He demanded that the bribery scandal be investigated and resolved, the sooner the better, and he also turned his attention toward the casinos. A security videotape surfaced of three men leaving one of the casino counting rooms carrying duffel bags assumed to be full of cash. Again, the media pounced on it and again the governor weighed in. "We can't have these 'goons' skimming profits from the casinos and just brazenly walking out the door with money that the State of Nevada should be collecting taxes on." He ordered the immediate revocation of that casino's license and its doors were closed, putting two thousand people out of work. But his private polling numbers moved up by six points.

It was a big story in Nevada but unfortunately for the governor hardly warranted a blip of attention on the national level. However, it did attract the attention of the board of directors for Eroe who recognized an expansion opportunity when it arose. The board chairman, Jerry Chapman, addressed the other members. "I think we simply apply to expand our license to include that property. We've never had any problems with the Gaming Commission, so I don't see why it wouldn't be approved." The others more or less agreed and the chief financial officer said there was more than enough money available to finance the acquisition. When Vince was alive he had always joked with Jack that the Board didn't even have one member with an ethnic name. They could have all stepped off the Mayflower, he said many times.

So, with all these distractions, Bruce and Greg were free to carry on their usual fraudulent ways. Not only were they still in business, they were able to hire new employees and were thinking about adding another couple trailers to the Pahrump Place compound. Money was always an issue, however. Therefore when the Desert Springs Hospital called about picking up a potential new client who was carrying close to twenty grand in cash, Bruce couldn't get there fast enough.

The case manager met Bruce in her office. "Such a strange case," she started. "We don't really know what happened to him. He was just dropped off on our doorstep, literally. He refuses to talk." She threw her hands up in frustration. "We treated a broken ankle and some broken ribs, but we don't know how he got any of his injuries." She knew Bruce would be intrigued by the other detail. "And, he has the most bizarre tattoo on his chest." She showed him a picture on her iPad of Jack's "instructions."

Bruce thought to himself, "He might as well have had our address tattooed on his chest, too." What he said was, "Poor soul. We'll just have to be gentle with him and see if one day he wants to tell us about this trauma." When the case manager handed him the paperwork and the envelope of cash, he looked serious. "We'll take good care of it, I mean, of him." He pulled the van around to the emergency room entrance and Jack was loaded in unceremoniously. For now they would simply call him JD, for John Doe, obviously. "The vultures," Jack thought silently.

The Eroe board was beginning to wish they could find their reclusive owner, too. The Gaming Commission heard their application for expansion of their license to include the shuttered Strip property, but the governor decided to insert himself into the process. "We don't even know if this man is alive," he told the Commission, and of course, the press. "He has never appeared in person before this Commission, and I find that insulting and very, very questionable." The Commission found itself having to deny the application, at least temporarily, but the chairman did call the Eroe board chairman and ask him to appear at their next meeting, in person; they would convene a special session the following week.

On the day of the hearing media trucks lined the streets of Carson City surrounding the Gaming Commission offices, eager for the showdown between the governor and the reclusive casino owner, formerly America's Hero. What they got instead was the very bland chairman of the Eroe board, conservatively dressed and carrying a slim portfolio. The governor stayed away in his office, not wanting to be shown waiting for the elusive Jack Hamilton.

"Mr. Chairman, if it will please the Commission," the Eroe spokesman began. "Mr. Hamilton is not able to attend today." A murmur went through the room. "He sends his regrets but asks that you consider his application in good faith." He paused and looked down, considering his next move. "Mr. Hamilton is a very, very private person owing to grievous injuries he suffered years ago in Texas." He slid a couple of photographs out of his portfolio. "I doubt a handful of people have seen him since that time, and reluctantly, I will show you why."

The photos were grainy, having been developed from security videotape in the basement of the Eroe when Jack was selecting his new truck. They were powerful nonetheless. "I would ask the Commission members to examine these but return them to me. It's not my wish to cause Mr. Hamilton any embarrassment or discomfort, but I hope he will understand the need for this…show." The Commissioners were clearly uncomfortable with what they saw and passed the photos back quickly. They conferred amongst themselves, microphones turned off; one suggested calling the governor for his input but was overruled. He was the first to leave the chambers to talk to the media.

That night on the news the meeting was the lead story. The Commission delayed their vote, which was expected, but what was unexpected was the graphic description the overruled Commissioner gave the media of Jack's appearance. "Well, it was horrifying, absolutely horrifying what's become of him," the cameras captured the Commissioner's look of shock. "I mean he has one eye, has lost one leg and part of his arm, and otherwise is absolutely unrecognizable, covered everywhere in burn scars that are too terrible to even contemplate." He added solemnly. "He barely looks human."

Julie Ann watched the news in the employee break room and experienced a strange sensation. Didn't Hank say his partner was named Jack and had been missing? He had only said once that Jack had been in a fire, like dad, and now Julie wondered. Could their new patient be the same Jack? She picked up the phone to call Hank but then stopped. If Jack were alive, would Hank lose the airplane business? Hank was doing so well, working on the new plane he had named the Phoenix, and she hated to disrupt that. Still…

Greg was watching the news, too. He almost whooped out loud, but grabbed his jacket and flew out of the facility. He drove the sixty miles to Vegas in record time and ran into Bruce's office. "We've got our keeper!"

Hank was too busy to watch the news or anything else. After stewing about the plane/Jack situation for a few weeks, he contacted the owner of the flight simulator and arranged for a face-to-face meeting. The owner readily agreed to front Hank the money to build another prototype which they would then take to some of the southern California air shows to see what the market might be. If it took off, literally and figuratively, they would find a factory and begin to produce the plane on a larger scale. Hank agreed to split his eighty percent of the company equally with the other man.

Fortunately, Jack had left his detailed lists of parts and suppliers, but now Hank found himself running for parts and then building the plane by himself. It was exhausting, but at least it kept his mind off the past.

Chapter Forty-Six

Bruce and Greg watched the ten o'clock news and were fully convinced that they had Jack Hamilton in their nursing home and within their grasp. "Move him to a private room and put a sign on the door to keep people out," Bruce ordered Greg. "Like quarantine, or something, whatever."

"Why?"

"Because we don't want anyone seeing him and tipping off the media before we're ready." Bruce was exasperated with Greg's mental acuity. "Then get a hold of the attorney and draw up the custody papers pronto. We need to get before a judge tomorrow."

Greg finally caught on. "Oh, right." As always, he had been thinking too small, just planning on extorting some money from Jack.

Jack wondered why he was suddenly being shunted into a private part of the complex and heard Greg warning everyone to stay out of John Doe's room. He didn't think he had any open wounds that might be contagious, but there must have been some reason for the hurried transfer. He still said nothing.

Greg got all the paperwork going the following morning and that afternoon he and Bruce were in court before a judge who had "worked with them" on previous similar cases. He raised an eyebrow when he saw the name on the custody petition. "Jack

Hamilton? The same Jack Hamilton that's the president of Eroe and their other casinos?"

"Well, I can't imagine that it is," Bruce replied, looking genuinely surprised. "I'm sure someone from the casino would have come forward to care for him." Then he looked pensive. "But that's a tough world, those casinos. They clearly just don't care about the poor man." Greg nodded in agreement but per their early arrangement said nothing.

"This seems highly unusual," the judge said hesitantly. "But I know you gentlemen have done this many times before." He signed the papers and motioned for his bailiff to hand them to Bruce who was fighting every impulse he had to laugh out loud. "Be sure you take good care of America's Hero," the judge warned.

"Oh, we will, we certainly will, your honor," Greg said, frustrated at not being allowed to say more.

When the two partners were outside, Greg asked Bruce, "So, what do we do with him now? We just waltz him into the casino and say, hey, we've got your owner, and by the way, can you validate our parking ticket?"

"You really are a moron," Bruce replied testily. "We inform them in advance that Mr. Hamilton will be returning to the hotel under our care and supervision, and would they make his suite ready as well as suites for us. Period."

"So we get to stay in the hotel overnight in a suite?" Greg asked eagerly. "I've always wanted to. Maybe I'll ask that gal from the convenience store…"

Bruce cut him off. "We don't stay overnight. We stay. Forever." And he added, "Forget that hag from the market. Once we're in Eroe and in charge we can have any woman we want."

They drove back to Pahrump in high spirits, Greg thinking about beautiful women, Bruce thinking about the power they would soon have. He left his coat and tie on despite the searing heat, thinking it would make him feel more professional when he called the casino. He decided to call the head of security first but was transferred several times. He could tell the people at Eroe thought it was a hoax. Finally, an administrative assistant came on the line. "I understand you have Mr. Hamilton in your care?" he asked.

"Yes, we do. We've been taking very fine care of him since his…accident," Bruce said officiously. "Now, however, he would like to return to Eroe, which he considers his home, and we are very supportive of that."

The assistant hesitated. "Perhaps it would be easier if we were to send one of our limos to pick up Mr. Hamilton. After all, it is a rather long drive for you from Pahrump, isn't it?"

"Not at all. We have a very comfortable van to transport Mr. Hamilton in, and, of course, my partner and I as well." Bruce didn't want to leak the entire extent of his plan until they were firmly ensconced in the grand suite that he was expecting. "So, shall we say in about three hours? You can have Mr. Hamilton's usual suite ready by then?"

The assistant sounded dubious but finally agreed. "Just come to parking garage number four, the underground level, and ask for Davis in security. He'll escort you and Mr. Hamilton to his suite." When he put the phone down, he called security and told them to be on the lookout for a van from Pahrump Place and to "inspect the contents very, very carefully."

Bruce put his phone down and turned to give Greg a high-five. "We're in like Flynn. Now let's go tell Mr. Doe it's been a pleasure having him as our guest, but now it's time to go home." They both laughed uproariously.

When Jack heard the door to his room open he thought, "Finally, I've been left here for hours with nothing to drink or eat or anything." The two men who entered were in suits and ties, clearly not medical attendants.

"Okay, Mr. Doe, or should we call you Mr. Hamilton?" the better-dressed one asked. "It's time to take you back where you belong, a sweet spot, I might say."

Greg laughed at the pun. "Sweet, suite, that's a good one."

Jack was dumbfounded that they discovered his identity and that they planned to return him to Eroe. Maybe if he failed to acknowledge them, they'd decide they were wrong? He looked straight ahead, but Bruce unlatched the safety brakes on his wheelchair and told Greg to get the door. He was wheeled out a back entrance to the nursing home and into the back of a van, the chair locked into place. Apparently he was going to Las Vegas.

Chapter Forty-Seven

No one was sure how it happened but the media found out about Jack's transfer and the Review Journal's headline was, "Jack's Back," in sixty-four-point type. There was an indistinct photo of a man in a wheelchair being put in a van, apparently being transferred from a hospital to a nursing home. The story was nothing but speculation about where the reclusive casino owner might have been for the past weeks and what, if anything, had happened to him.

Hank saw the headline when he stopped for coffee in Las Vegas on one of his many parts runs. He grabbed the newspaper and read quickly through the frustratingly vague story. At first he felt relief that his friend and partner was apparently safe. But it didn't take long for the relief to give way to anger. If he was this big-shot casino executive, why didn't Hank ever know about it? And why hasn't he contacted Hank all this time. Hank thought about the days and days he had spent combing the desert around the hangar in ever-widening circles looking for any sign of Jack or the plane, returning home every night sadder and more frustrated. Would he call Hank now? Should Hank call him?

But Jack was not going to be making any calls, that much was clear. Bruce and Greg were met in the parking garage by the security chief and his assistant who confirmed that their passenger was indeed Jack Hamilton, president of Eroe and the AHG. They gingerly lifted Jack in his wheelchair out of the grimy van and moved toward the elevator. Bruce jumped out of the driver's seat, however, and motioned for Greg to get out of the van as well. "Just a minute," Bruce said in his most commanding tone. "We will be accompanying Mr. Hamilton to his suite."

The security chief didn't let go of the wheelchair and said quite definitely, "We were not advised of that arrangement."

"Well you're advised of it now."

The two security men looked uneasy but one picked up a radio and spoke to Jack's administrative assistant waiting upstairs. He wasn't happy with the answer he received but held the elevator doors open for the two men from Pahrump and signaled for another guard to move the van to a parking place. All four men rode up to the thirtieth floor, surrounding Jack in the elevator, no one saying a word. When the elevator doors opened again, they revealed a gleaming honey-colored marble hallway paneled in rich cherry wood, leading to a set of double doors that opened as soon as the elevator doors closed again. Jack's administrative assistant stood waiting, clearly pleased to see Jack but obviously annoyed at the two intruders.

Greg had to fight to keep himself from gawking when they entered the suite with its floor-to-ceiling windows and lavish golden yellow furnishings. He pushed Jack's wheelchair over to one of the windows. "Now, isn't that nice, Mr. Hamilton, you'll be able to sit here and watch the planes take off and land," he said in a smarmy tone.

"Yeah, you asshole, why don't you see if they can put an oil derrick out there, too, for me to look at. Oh, and have the TV set to run my movie continuously." Jack kept his thoughts to himself but almost choked when he heard Bruce's pronouncement.

Bruce pulled some legal papers out of his suit coat pocket and handed them to the assistant. "You will see from these court documents that we," and he motioned to Bruce who was still staring out the window, "have complete custodial care of Mr. Hamilton, and that includes all of his financial matters and any interests he has in any properties, including obviously, this hotel."

"Jack, is this true?" the assistant moved toward his boss.

"He doesn't speak apparently," Bruce answered. "And, it doesn't matter if he decides to because the matter is done." The assistant was livid, but Bruce pushed on. "Now, if you will get two adjoining suites ready for me and my colleague, we'll be settling in."

"I'm sure our legal team will have something to say about this," the assistant huffed.

"Just tell them to make an appointment with me and let them know what suite I'll be *living* in." The angry young man looked beseechingly in Jack's direction, but Bruce showed him to the door.

Downstairs, the hotel's call center was overloaded with callers, particularly reporters, asking to speak to Mr. Hamilton. Hank was one of the callers trying to get through but none of his explanations of his relationship with Jack permeated the call center staff's strict instructions to keep all calls away from the suite. Hank left Las Vegas dejected and thought about driving out to Pahrump to see his mother. He called her instead. "Did you hear," he asked her, "my partner, Jack, is back, and he's actually the president of Eroe, that big hotel?"

"Oh Hank, I know, have known," Julie Ann stuttered. "I mean I know they brought him in here a few days ago and then moved him out all hush-hush..."

Hank almost shouted into the phone, "You knew my partner was right there and you didn't tell me!"

"I wanted to, but I thought..."

"You didn't think anything and you never do!" Hank was shouting by now.

"I didn't want you to lose your airplane business just because he was alive!" Julie Ann shouted back.

"That's crap! Jack wouldn't have done that." Hank was too angry to continue the conversation and just ended the call.

As angry as Hank was, Jack was twice that. He watched the two buffoons sprawl out on the couches and call demands down to room service for food and drinks, champagne, no less! He hoped the hotel did give them their own suites so at least they would leave his. He recognized that he was too angry at the moment to clearly analyze the situation, but he would. There had to be a way to work this to his advantage, and if there was, he'd find it soon enough.

Chapter Forty-Eight

Eroe did provide two suites for Bruce and Greg, which did afford Jack more privacy. After that first day they rarely even looked in on him, which suited Jack just fine. Fortunately when his two captors, and that's how he thought of them, had looked through the suite, they didn't discover Jack's hidden surveillance room. Jack was able to wheel himself in there and watch the resort casino operations quite closely. And, with a camera aimed at the private elevator to his suite, he always had plenty of warning if either of the men was planning a visit.

At first, all Greg did was tour the casino's restaurants, gorging himself on the now-free food and drinks, pawing the cocktail waitresses (who had been alerted to both his and Bruce's new roles), and generally making an ass out of himself. Casino staff were certainly well used to drunk and obnoxious patrons, but ones you couldn't say no to? It rankled them and it drove Jack's blood pressure up to watch the spectacle they made.

Bruce was by far the more serious threat, Jack soon observed. He was shocked and saddened to watch and listen in to the meeting with his legal staff and board members in the main conference room. Initially, Bruce was met with a token amount of protests from the lawyers questioning the custodial agreements, but those soon were squelched by the board members, the chairman in particular.

"You know, gentlemen, as distressed and saddened as we are about Mr. Hamilton's condition, it does give us a certain…opportunity, shall we say." He had everyone's attention. "We now have a person," gesturing toward Bruce, "who controls Mr. Hamilton's interests and therefore those of Eroe and the AHG, and who could," and here he hesitated only slightly, "appear before the gaming commission to request the expansion that they have so far tabled." Jack could see that Bruce looked like a peacock in full feather. With only a cursory discussion of the proposal, another member called for a vote on the idea, and it was unanimous. Bruce would represent Eroe at the next commission meeting. "I'll forward a copy of the custodial agreement in advance to the commission," the board chairman said, "so that there are no surprises."

Greedy bastards," Jack thought, watching the video feed. But after he thought about the action, he realized that Bruce was only digging himself in deeper while, at least, Eroe would be expanding and that could only benefit everyone, himself included, when he regained control—and he was certain he would.

So, when Jack wasn't ensconced in his surveillance room, he sat placidly in his wheelchair, but not looking out at the airport, talking to himself. All those hours and hours of voice training for his movie role were going to pay off. Within a few days he was certain he had mastered Bruce's nasal delivery and decided to put it to the test. He phoned the main casino cage. "This is Bruce Barnes. Will you please send ten thousand dollars in hundred dollar bills to my suite? Just leave it in an envelope on the table in the foyer." He was gratified to hear a, "Right away, Mr. Barnes," in response, and a few minutes later he heard the suite door open then close again quite quickly.

Why not have some fun with it, Jack thought? He called the central kitchen. Mimicking Greg's slobbery drawl he asked, "Will you instruct the wait staff tonight to bill everyone's dinner in the steak house to me? This is Greg Nelson. Just have it put on my tab, will you?" Once again, Jack got a speedy, "Yes, sir." So, every few days he instructed that another ten thousand dollars be delivered to the suite, and he waited for the inevitable clash between Bruce and Greg.

He didn't have to wait long. He watched the two men in Bruce's suite, to which Bruce had summoned Greg. "Just how big a loser are you?" Bruce said, pointing his finger into Greg's chest. "Buying two hundred steak dinners one night, then comping the entire showroom the next?" Greg looked bewildered, but as Jack had observed, that was nothing new. Bruce continued his tirade against his partner until finally Greg had had enough.

"At least I don't have my hand in the till," Greg countered. "I know about the money you've been taking."

"So I get a few hundred dollars here and there. What about it?"

"I think it's a lot more than that," Greg stammered, red in the face from being angry and humiliated. "And I don't know what you're talking about, dinners and showroom shit. So, I've brought a couple of friends in from Pahrump and treated them to dinner. Big f-in deal."

But Bruce was not to be mollified. "And that's another thing. Here we're finally in a position of respect and power and you drag those trailer trash friends of yours in from Pahrump!" Bruce opened the door to his suite and virtually pushed Greg out of it. "I'm telling you—you better clean up your act buddy, or you're out! In fact, that's a great idea. Why don't you go back out to Pahrump and just concentrate on running the home, instead of leaving somebody in charge who's worked for us for what, two weeks, to do it?" Bruce privately thought that Julie Ann was about ten times sharper than Greg, but that wasn't the point in this argument.

Greg left without saying another word and went downstairs, pulling up a stool at the first bar he came to. It didn't take long before he was slurring his words, talking to anyone who would listen. Of course, Jack was upstairs listening. "I could kill that bastard! Who the hell does he think he is dictating to me!" And on and on. The bartender tried to gradually slow down his service so that Greg wouldn't notice, but he demanded the bottle of Jack

Daniels be placed in front of him so he could pour his own shots. After about two hours, Greg had company. A middle-aged man with a gray ponytail, dressed in an army fatigue jacket and well-worn jeans pulled up the stool next to Greg, who immediately offered him a shot, and then another.

"So, pardner, who's got you so riled up today?" the stranger asked, pouring himself another shot.

"Oh, it's my asshole partner, my big college buddy, bigshot executive," Greg said, tossing back another. "Thinks he owns the place." He started to laugh. "Maybe he does own the place. He's still an asshole."

Jack was ready to stop listening, but then it got interesting. "Well, people like that can always be put in their place, you know what I mean?" Greg's new friend said slyly.

"Yeah, and what place would that be?" Greg slurred.

"Could be someplace out in the desert," the man said, moving closer to Greg, "someplace where nobody would see him again." He slid a piece of paper toward Greg, who stuffed it in his pocket without looking at it. "You need that kind of help, you call me, bud."

"Well, I just might." Then gaining more determination. "I just might, all right." The two drained the last of the bottle of Jack Daniels. The stranger slipped away while a security guard came to

Greg's side and suggested he might want to go up to his suite. Greg let himself be led away. Jack watched and listened, then switched monitors to see Greg being let into his suite where he promptly passed out.

Chapter Forty-Nine

Bruce never ventured into Jack's suite, delegating the responsibility for checking on him to Greg, who dreaded it more each time. "I hate the way he stares at me with that one eye," he complained to Bruce. "And why doesn't he have a patch over the other one? It creeps me out."

"I think that's the price you pay for the lifestyle you have," Bruce sneered. "You would never have even seen the inside of a suite like that except for him," jerking his thumb in the direction of Jack's suite. "You thought a room at the Pahrump Nugget with a vibrating bed was a big deal."

Greg could feel his blood pressure rising at the constant put-downs he endured from Bruce. "Yeah? I remember your tongue hanging out at the thought of riding in a limo," he lashed back. "I don't know why we can't just put him someplace, or kill him, for that matter."

"Kill him? Did you just say something that stupid?" Bruce shook his head. "He dies and we're out of here so fast it'd make your head spin." He decided he finally had to 'educate' Greg on their situation. "While gorging yourself at the buffet or pounding down the cocktails, I'm in meetings with the legal staff here, for your information."

"Oh yeah, because you're such a bigshot."

"Sit down and listen to me," Bruce said. "When that creep, as you call him, first built Eroe he and his manager at the time had a little trouble with the mob from back East." Jack, meanwhile, was listening intently to this story from his surveillance room. "Jack got the mob by telling them that if anything happened to him, the whole kit and caboodle would go to the Catholic Church here in Vegas."

Greg burst out laughing. "What the hell?"

"It's in his will."

"So what do we do, become priests?"

By now Bruce was laughing, too. "Yeah, I could see that. No, we keep him very much alive and well while we see just how much we can skim off the top."

"I thought that was illegal?" Greg began.

"Of course it's illegal. When has that ever been a problem for you?" Bruce was becoming exasperated again by his slow-witted accomplice. "It doesn't mean it can't be done. All we need are friends in the right places, the counting room in particular." Greg still looked confused. "I'm working on making those friends and pretty soon we'll be rolling in it." He hated to do it, but he confided in Greg. "I've set up an account for us that has almost a half a mil in it already."

"When were you planning on telling me about that?" Greg asked indignantly. "Christmas?"

"I was going to tell you when I got a few more pieces of the plan in place, but that's going to happen very soon, trust me."

"I guess I don't have any choice, do I?" Greg wasn't half as stupid as Bruce thought. "I guess I'll just let you build up our little nest egg."

Jack was ready to call down to the casino cage and have everyone fired, but he was also interested to see how this would play out.

"I still hate how he just sits there and stares at me when I come in the room," Greg whined. "Why can't we just put him back in a room at Pahrump Place or somewhere?"

Bruce thought he might have to give Greg this concession. "Well, maybe you've got something there. This suite could bring in big bucks from the high rollers." He appeared to hesitate. "But we can't put him out in Pahrump. I think we'd have to convince the powers-that-be here that it would be better if he were receiving the *rehabilitative care* that only a high-end facility could provide." Bruce laughed. "I think we could find a place like that to park our friend." He stood up to dismiss Greg. "I'll work on it." They shook hands and Greg left Bruce's suite.

Greg headed back to his own suite and while patting his pockets looking for his key, he came across the piece of paper the guy at the bar yesterday had given him. Even though he had been thoroughly hammered, he remembered the guy had been interesting to talk to. Maybe he'd give him a call, see if he wanted to come down and hit one of the other bars in the resort. The paper just said 'Gus' and gave a phone number. He cleaned up a bit and made the call. "Hey, Gus, man, it's Greg Nelson down at Eroe. We had a few shots yesterday."

"Yeah, man, I remember you." Gus sounded half-asleep even though it was late afternoon.

"So, anyway, if you're not doing anything later I thought you might come back down, we'll hit one of the other bars, maybe get a bite, whatever." Greg added, "On me, of course."

"Now you're talkin'." Gus seemed more awake. "I'll come down around seven, look for you at that bar that looks over the pool, check out the talent, you know what I mean?"

"Oh yeah, I know what you mean bro," Greg drawled. "See you then."

With three hours to kill, Greg thought he might as well check on Jack one more time. The only other person allowed in the suite was the administrative assistant who presumably saw to it that his meals were delivered and he was cleaned up every day. At least Greg didn't have to attend to that chore. He took the elevator up to the suite and found Jack, as usual, sitting by the window, although he did turn in his wheelchair to study Greg when he entered. Now that he knew that his staring bothered Greg, Jack was determined to do it every chance he got.

"So, Jack, maybe we'll put you in one of those planes you're so fascinated by pretty soon," Greg taunted him, wondering if Jack understood anything at all but rather doubting it. "Or maybe load you in one of those limos for a road trip. Hasta la vista, baby." Naturally, Jack said nothing, so Greg was ready to beat his retreat. "Nice to see you're still alive. Catch you later." He made his exit; Jack was tempted to spit on him on his way out but restrained himself.

Chapter Fifty

At the end of the day when it was time to relax with a beer, Hank thought about Jack and wondered why he hadn't called. It must be the demands of running the big resort, Hank thought, but then had to admit that when Jack had been at the hangar, somebody must have been running things then. He worried that Jack was somehow sick or injured, especially after seeing the photo of him in a wheelchair that had been splashed all over the newspapers. His mother could have told him, but Hank would be damned if he'd call her.

For his part, Jack ached to call Hank and find out how his young protégé was doing. But, he couldn't risk any record of an outgoing phone call from his suite when he wasn't supposed to be able to talk. Nor could he get on the internet and order a cell phone without its delivery raising the same concerns. He would bide his time.

Bruce was biding his time as well, waiting to fully implement his skimming plan. He hadn't told Greg the entire truth about the money he had already extracted. In fact, it was entirely in an account in Greg's name, so if anyone were to be caught, it would all fall on him. As he wandered through the casino he was relieved to see that Greg seemed to have made a new friend; at least he'd be less of an irritation for a while. He did have to admit, however, that Greg's suggestion of moving Jack somewhere else was a good one. Bruce sensed that Jack knew more about what was going on around him than anyone believed, and it might be wise to get him off the property.

By running Pahrump Place, Bruce had become a member of a nursing home association and he vividly remembered how the high-end facilities directors had turned their noses up at him at one of their annual meetings. Now might be the perfect time to contact one of them, however. He called the administrator of Newport Shores who he remembered as being particularly icy to him. When the woman finally came on the line, she was as haughty as he remembered. "Oh, yes, Mr. Barnes. I do seem to remember something about a little trailer facility you ran. Where was it? Somewhere in the desert?"

"Pahrump."

"Oh, yes, Pahrump. Who could forget?"

Bruce forced himself to be pleasant. "Well, you did." He laughed but she didn't. "Actually, I'm calling about a patient we have who might really benefit from a long-term stay at your facility."

She almost started to laugh. "You do realize, Mr. Barnes, that our rates start at five thousand dollars a week, and that's for just the most basic care." She sneered, "I doubt anyone who found themselves in your little facility could begin to afford that."

"Oh, our client can afford the top-of-the-line care," Bruce said unctuously. "That's why I thought of

Newport Shores first." He waited a beat. "We were thinking of about twenty thousand a week." He heard her gasp. "Would that cover it then?"

She was flustered but wasn't about to let this opportunity slide away. "Certainly, certainly it would."

"Well, then it's settled. We'll deliver him tomorrow," Bruce fairly purred. "Oh, and we'll bring a check for a month in advance, too." When they hung up he added, "Bitch."

Jack had been listening to all of Bruce's calls all along and smiled broadly at this new development. So he was going to Newport Beach, huh?

Bruce roamed around the casino looking for Greg to give him the good news and found him at the pool bar with his new friend. "Hey, Greg, got to talk to you for a sec," he said, taking Greg's arm, not bothering to acknowledge the other man. When he had pulled him a few feet away he kept his hand on Greg's arm. "Listen, don't get shit-faced tonight. We've got a job to do tomorrow."

Greg immediately became indignant and pulled his arm away. "I don't think…" Gus was at his side instantly, glaring at Bruce.

"The man was having a drink, buddy," Gus said quietly to Bruce. "He'll talk to you when he's ready."

"Yeah, and who are you, his new big brother?" Bruce glared back.

"Okay, okay, guys," Greg was getting nervous. "I'll just talk to my partner here for a minute, Gus. Get us another couple drinks and I'll be right back." Gus walked back to the bar but not without first giving Bruce the once-over, his smirk suggesting that he wasn't impressed.

"Christ, where'd you find that loser? Another Pahrump pal?" Bruce shook his head. "Listen, tomorrow we're going to Newport Beach, first thing in the morning. We're taking Jack to a facility there." Greg smiled. "So, now you're happy?"

"Yeah, that's cool with me," Greg acknowledged. The two worked out the details of when to load Jack into one of the company's limos, and Bruce left Greg to rejoin his drinking buddy, with the admonition not to show up drunk in the morning. Jack watched the pool bar monitor and was amused at the interchange. The gambler in him wouldn't bet on Greg showing up sober.

Gus was enjoying himself watching the topless part of the resort pool. Definitely some fine-looking ladies still sipping their tropical drinks even though it was getting close to eight o'clock. "Gotta love this desert heat," he said to Greg. "Those babes will be here till midnight."

Greg puffed up. "Yeah, if they're not in my suite."

"So you're some kind of high-roller or what here?"

"No, better than that," Greg explained. "Me and my partner there, we basically control the place." Gus looked impressed. "Actually, we control the guy that owns the place but he's like gorked-out, can't talk and just sits upstairs all day looking out the window. It's weird."

"Yeah, that is weird." Gus poured them both another drink. "But you shouldn't let your partner push you around like that. Man's gotta be a man, you know."

"Oh, he's just that way. I've known him for years, never changes." Greg took a big swallow of the whiskey. "I just act dumb and then do whatever I want to do anyway." He laughed and Gus laughed along with him, but only for a minute.

"Still, dude. You gotta get tired of that treatment after a while. I know I would." A particularly stunning specimen climbed out of the pool and Gus was too busy staring to continue his train of thought. The two men continued to drink and drool until well past midnight when Gus finally said it was time for him to leave. Greg offered to send him home in one of the Eroe limos or at least pay for a cab, but Gus declined. As he left, he handed Greg his card. "So, call me when you're back from your little errand and we'll talk."

Greg was swaying on his feet but took Gus's card and said he'd call in a day or two. He made his way to the elevator and on the way up took a look at the card. Three lines. Gus Jacobs, a phone number, and "Deeds Done."

Chapter Fifty-One

Surprisingly, Greg was at Jack's suite promptly at eight the next morning, ready to take Jack down to the waiting limo. Bruce stopped by the suite, prepared to wait and give Greg yet another lecture; instead he held the door as Greg wheeled Jack out to the elevator. One of Eroe's signature stretch gray limos was parked at the base of the elevator, motor running, air conditioning cranked up. The driver lifted Jack out of his chair and placed him in the back seat, carefully buckling him in, then put the wheelchair in the trunk. The driver left Bruce and Greg to fend for themselves, but much to his annoyance, Greg climbed in the front passenger seat, leaving Bruce with Jack. It was about a five-hour drive to the coast and Greg made numerous attempts at conversation with the driver, who was just as responsive as Jack. Bruce worked on his laptop and everyone else stared out their respective windows.

The limo's navigation system directed them easily to Newport Shores. Greg couldn't help but whistle when they pulled into a lushly landscaped circular driveway set off by a fountain with patinated copper seals and dolphins. The Mediterranean-style building had a two-story lobby and several wings stretching off each side, all with views of the ocean. As soon as the limo came to a stop, an attendant stepped forward to open the rear door while the driver popped the hatch for the trunk. Another attendant retrieved the wheelchair and settled Jack into it. "And this is Mr. Hamilton, I presume," the attendant said to Bruce.

"Yes, it is. Let's get him inside, shall we?"

The administrator waited in the lobby to greet them personally. "I trust you had a pleasant drive," she addressed Bruce, ignoring Greg who had a large coffee stain on the front of his shirt, the result of the driver braking a little too abruptly at one point. "We have Mr. Hamilton's room all ready for him, if you'll just follow me."

No other residents were in sight as they followed the administrator down the carpeted hallways, and even Greg noted the facility had none of the smells associated with a nursing home. She opened the door to a very pleasant sitting room with a small outdoor patio and a bedroom already equipped with a hospital bed. "I think Mr. Hamilton will be more than comfortable here." The attendant pushed Jack's wheelchair toward the window, but noting his burns, kept him out of the direct sun.

"Well, this looks just fine," Bruce said. "I'm sure in six months or a year he'll be back to new." Greg laughed but stopped at a searing looks from Jack. "Poor soul, as I explained in our phone conversation, can't speak and we really don't know if he understands anything that goes on around him." He took the administrator's hand and in his most sincere performance added, "I'm sure you can provide him everything he needs, and, God willing, return him to us a new man."

They left Jack with an attendant who locked the brakes on Jack's chair and poured a glass of water from a crystal decanter on a side table. He patted Jack gently on the shoulder. "Don't worry about a thing, Mr. Hamilton."

"I'm not worried at all," Jack said. "In fact, get notebook. I've got a list of things I need."

The attendant stammered, "But they said..."

"Forget what those assholes said. Just do what I ask, please." He unlocked the brakes and swiveled to face the man. "And let's keep it between you and I for now."

The man gave a sharp salute, having already been briefed on Jack's history as America's hero. "I'm on it, sir."

Bruce and Greg settled a few details with the administrator then made their way back to the limo. The driver opened the door for Bruce but left Greg standing on the opposite side of the car to open his own door. Greg made a note to remember this guy's name. "Well, that went well," Bruce said to the back of Greg's head. "Now we can really get down to business." The sleek limo pulled away from Jack's new home.

Jack was already dictating his list. "I need a laptop computer, a good one with plenty of power. We have WiFi here?" The attendant nodded in the affirmative.

"I need a cell phone, any kind. Put about two hundred minutes on it for now." He added some miscellaneous items then reached in the pocket of his robe where he had secreted the regular "withdrawals" he had made in Bruce's voice at the casino. "Here's three grand. That should get you started." He saluted the attendant. "Dismissed, for now." Jack had to admit that he was exhausted from the boring drive and the tension of the situation. A nap would be good.

He awoke a few hours later to a beautiful sunset over the ocean and the attendant setting out his dinner. "I think you'll prefer dinner here rather than the communal dining room." Jack agreed and saw that the dinner looked very good, which it was. He even had a glass of wine. Tomorrow would be a busy day.

The next morning the attendant, who Jack learned was named Scottie, woke Jack and helped him into a handicapped-accessible shower. He also had laid out the clothes Jack had requested on his list instead of a hospital gown and robe. The laptop sat on his desk, the cell phone next to it. A light fog bank lingered so Jack allowed himself to sit out on the patio and breathe in the refreshing ocean air. Breakfast was simple but filling.

"You know, sir, they'll want you to go down for therapy at some point," Scottie said tentatively.

"Tell them I'm too sick from the car ride yesterday. I'll figure something else out later."

"Will do, sir." Scottie excused himself and left Jack to work.

Jack used the laptop to find the phone number he needed. "Dr. Eric Knight, please."

"Dr. Knight is in surgery," the receptionist answered. "May I take a message?"

"Yes, tell him Jack Hamilton needs him on the double. I'm at the...what is the name of this place...Newport Shores. Here's my cell phone number." She repeated it back to Jack. "Have him call me as soon as he's free."

A few hours went by during which Jack was able to establish a connection to the surveillance system at Eroe. He was definitely going to be keeping an eye on 'the boys' to see what they would do next.

His cell phone rang, playing the Star Spangled Banner. Jack thought about Scottie programming it in. Everyone's a comedian. "Jack Hamilton here."

"It's Eric. What are you doing in a rest home in Newport?"

"Oh, just taking the air, you know." He chuckled but got serious quickly. "Listen, I need another arm just like the last one."

"What do you mean, the last one? What happened to it?" the orthopedic surgeon asked. "That was one-of-a-kind."

"It's buried out in the Mojave. Trust me, it's a long story."

The surgeon laughed, too. "Man, you are the luckiest unlucky man I've ever met. I'll have to come out and take some new measurements, maybe…let's see, how about Thursday?"

"I'm not going anywhere," Jack agreed. "If you get a sooner cancellation, that's good, too." Before the surgeon could hang up, Jack added, "Oh, and I need a leg, too."

"Same one?"

"Yes, same one!" Everybody's a comedian.

Chapter Fifty-Two

It was late by the time Bruce and Greg got back to Las Vegas, and although the allure of the bars was strong, even Greg said he was going straight to his room to catch up on his sleep. Bruce said he planned to do the same but first had to meet with the reservations center and the pit bosses to see about renting out Jack's grand suite as soon as the appropriate high-roller "whale" could be hooked. He gave Greg his laptop and asked him to drop it at his room on the way.

Greg let himself into Bruce's suite and started to drop the laptop off on the foyer table. He couldn't understand what Bruce was always doing on the thing. They had long ago hired an accountant to do the bookkeeping for Pahrump Place; Greg had slept through most of his accounting classes in college and Bruce considered it 'grunt work.' So, out of curiosity, Greg made himself a drink from Bruce's wet bar and sat down to scroll through the screens. What he found astounded him.

The bank account that Bruce had told him about with supposedly a half a million dollars in it for both of them instead bore only Greg's name and it had almost three million dollars in it. Greg copied down the account information and quickly closed up the laptop. He took the drink with him back to his room and spent most of the rest of the night turning over the possibilities in his mind. He should have looked to see if there was another account in Bruce's name alone, but after thinking about it, he realized there wouldn't be. Bruce was clearly skimming money out of Eroe, but he was setting Greg up to be the fall guy if the scheme was discovered. If it wasn't, then at some point Bruce would simply add his own name to the account—or maybe he'd take Greg's off and do a disappearing act with the money. Finally sheer fatigue took over and Greg slept, but fitfully at that.

Jack, on the other hand, slept better than he had in years with the sound of the ocean coming in through the patio doors and the cool breezes. He was ready to make another of his famous lists. Buy house by ocean. Have all French doors. Install fountains. Have covered loggia. He continued to monitor Eroe remotely, but it didn't appear that any big moves were imminent. Jack still felt he had more to fear from Bruce than from Greg, but that's where he was wrong.

Greg finally got up around noon and decided to call his friend Gus, but got his answering machine instead. "Hey, it's Greg. Give me a call if you want to do something. You've got my number. See ya!" He spent the remainder of the afternoon in his room, even ordering room service instead of making the rounds of the restaurants. There had to be something he could do about Bruce, the money, the whole thing. Maybe Gus would have an idea if the guy would ever call back.

About five o'clock Gus did call and said he'd come down to Eroe in an hour or so, but this time Greg invited him to his suite. He had room service send up some snacks and refresh the in-room bar. Jack watched all this on the remote surveillance feed and thought, "Jeez, are they dating or what?" Jack noted Bruce was in the casino cage chatting up one of the tellers. "That figures."

Gus knocked on the door to the suite, not really expecting anything more than an ordinary hotel room. When Greg opened the door and stepped back, Gus immediately reacted. "Whoa, dude, what a set-up!" He walked to the windows overlooking The Strip while Greg mixed them both a drink. "I guess you're in control of this place all right."

"Yeah, it's pretty sweet isn't it? Get it? Sweet/suite?" Greg gushed.

"I get it, I get it." They talked about the weather, sports, the drive to Newport Beach, and other trivia.

After another round of drinks, Greg pulled out Gus' business card. "Deeds done? So what's up with that? What kind of deeds?"

"Oh, just odd jobs sort of, helping people with situations."

"Situations?"

"Yeah, if somebody has something they can't take care of themselves, you know, I take care of it for them." He could see Greg didn't understand.

"Haven't you ever heard the song by AC/DC, 'Dirty Deeds Done Dirt Cheap'?"

"I love that song, man," Greg said and sang a few bars of it. "So what, for example?"

"For the last three days I've been cleaning out a garage for a lady whose husband died. That guy must've saved everything he ever touched. What a load of crap." Gus swore. "I've made about eight trips out to the county dump, but she's payin' for it, so it's all good for Gus."

"That's cool," Greg said tentatively.

"When I got out of the Army, there wasn't much call for my specialty, so I'm open to anything that pays the bills, pretty much."

"What was your specialty?"

Gus took a big swallow of his whisky. "I was a sniper, one of the best."

Greg almost dropped his drink. "So you killed people?"

"Well that is what snipers do. Yeah, I killed a bunch of people before they tried to kill us." He set his drink down. "It used to bother me, but not so much anymore."

The wheels were turning so fast in Greg's mind that he thought his head might explode. "So, you still shoot? Go out to a range or something?"

"I do. Now it sort of calms me." Gus laughed. "Got to keep your skills up. Never know when the Chinese or some other assholes might decide to invade us."

Greg decided to test the waters. "So you actually could do a dirty deed then, too…"

Gus looked at him closely. "Depends."

"On?"

Gus hesitated. "On how bad somebody wants one done. How much they'd be willing to pay. How it could be done clean, you know?"

"Oh, yeah, yeah. I hear ya." He moved to make them both another drink and was almost relieved when room service arrived with an actual dinner. The men reverted to small talk over the meal, but Greg was still thinking of the possibilities.

Chapter Fifty-Three

Over the next few weeks Jack met with his orthopedic surgeon and received a new prosthetic leg. The arm was a bit more complicated and Dr. Knight told Jack it would take another week or so to build it and then Jack would have to "train" it like he did the previous one. "Patience, Jack, patience," the surgeon counseled him. "You could always go dig up the last one." Jack passed the time monitoring Eroe and actually did participate in some physical therapy trying to get his muscle tone back. Having the leg at least allowed him to get out of the wheelchair.

"Damn!" he blurted out in therapy when the leg slipped and he crashed to the floor. Everyone was surprised to hear him say anything. "Oh, the hell with it. Yes, I can talk. Yes, I know what's going on," he told the therapists. His 'confession' soon made it to the attention of the administrator who called on him in his room.

"Mr. Hamilton, it's wonderful that you've regained your faculties so quickly," she said doubtfully. "Would you like to explain what's going on?" She saw his reluctance, although he did greet her when she came in the room. "Perhaps I can call your, what are they, custodians, and tell them the good news."

That did it for Jack. "They're not my custodians, more like my captors." He told her the entire story. "It's my own damn fault. My pride and my disappointment just overwhelmed me and I let myself be carried along in the current." He shook his head. "Didn't know that current was leading to a cesspool."

She listened, fascinated by all that had happened. "Well, if you spent even five minutes in their care that was four too long." She promised to keep Jack's status a secret for the time being while he monitored the developments at Eroe and waited for his new arm.

At Eroe meanwhile, Gus and Greg continued their little dance, Greg asking a lot of "what if" questions and Gus being cagey, answering with "depends" more often than not. They both knew where their discussions were headed. Greg was watching the dollars pile up in Bruce's secret account for him, wondering when enough would be enough.

Bruce finally had the key players he needed on board in the casino's counting room so that the skim was running smoothly. Over the years he had become increasingly arrogant, but now he was virtually impossible, and his usual target was Greg. He belittled him every chance he got with comments about his increasing weight, his shabby wardrobe, his questionable friends and anything else he could think of. He hoped Greg would tire of it and simply leave, go back to managing Pahrump Place, or whatever. The woman they had hired, Julie Ann, was doing a competent job of keeping the residents cared for, but Bruce wished Greg would go back and take care of the business end of things. Greg had no such plans, however, and Bruce didn't realize the direction he was pushing him.

He approached Greg and Gus seated poolside at the topless pool. "So, those that can't do, watch huh? You two realize you'd never stand a chance with any of them don't you?" Bruce taunted them. "Why don't you pin some medals on that ratty Army jacket, Gus—that might impress the ladies." He laughed but Gus jumped out of his chair and grabbed Bruce's shirt front in one fluid motion.

"At least I served, and yes, I do have the medals to prove it!" His eyes never left Bruce's who was finally forced to look away. Gus released him with a warning. "You come around me again, or Greg, it better be respectfully."

"Or what?" Bruce sneered. "Don't forget who runs this place." He turned on his heel and left.

The confrontation was the proverbial straw that broke the camel's back. "I've gotta get rid of that son of a bitch," Greg swore. "I'm not puttin' up with him one more week." Plus, the millions that were in his account would be more than enough to keep him happy on a beach in Mexico for years to come.

"I hear ya. Don't know how you took it so long," Gus said, although he thought, he didn't know *why* Greg took it in the first place. The guy was kind of a slob but he was a straight-up guy and had treated Gus well, he thought. Maybe it was time to help him out. Jack was listening in, and yes, watching the topless sunbathers, but he wasn't prepared for the rest of the conversation. "You know, Greg, I could take care of that prick for you."

"How? Or I should say, how soon?"

"I wouldn't just shoot him on the street, but I think an accident could be arranged, shall we say." Greg leaned forward and encouraged him to continue. "I think if we could get him out on the freeway, I could shoot the tires out of his car, cause it to roll, and the rest would be history."

"That might take out a lot of other cars," Greg said thoughtfully. "I don't know…"

"Well, it could be out in the desert, you know, that long stretch out by Primm."

"I don't know how I'd get him out there's the thing."

"Well, you work on it, let me know." He signaled the cocktail waitress for another round and sent drinks over to two girls by the pool; they barely acknowledged Gus. "Timing is everything. Speaking of which, I've got to go to work." He left Greg deep in thought, having not even touched his last cocktail.

Greg watched Bruce make another circuit through the casino floor, pausing at the two-for-one roulette promotion and the idea came to him. It was genius.

Chapter Fifty-Four

"You're a genius, doc." Jack flexed the new arm and clicked the sides of the hook together. He still remembered how Hank laughed every time he used it to open a beer bottle. Just thinking about Hank made him feel sad and ashamed all over again. He needed to explain, if any explanation were indeed possible. "I see you've added something extra," laughing at the inscription the doctor had added, 'If found, return to Jack Hamilton.'

"Well, nobody loses the same arm twice but you, Jack." He tested a few of the nerve connection components. "Or the same leg, for that matter." The physical therapists were anxious to see just how much Jack could do with the titanium contraption, so Dr. Knight made Jack pick up small objects, sort them, and even catch a pen thrown to him. Every test went well and Jack was beaming. The doctor packed up his testing equipment and gave Jack a hearty handshake. "I don't want to see you again unless it's over a platter of ribs at that joint you run in Vegas."

Vegas. What was Jack going to do about returning to Las Vegas and taking control of Eroe again? He didn't think he could put it off much longer. His expression clouded, but he still managed to thank the surgeon who had also become his friend. "Ribs? Hell, you can have the whole damn pig!"

As it turned out, Jack couldn't put Vegas off at all. When he checked the recording from the previous night's surveillance of Greg and Bruce, he saw Greg once again huddled with Gus at the pool bar, but this time they didn't even appear to be watching the women. "I figured out how to get Bruce out on I-15," Greg was eagerly telling Gus. "And, I can make it even one better by having that creep Jack in the car with him." Gus listened intently, all the time eyeing a blue gym bag that Greg kept on the floor tightly wedged between his feet. "All I have to do is call the rehab facility in Newport and tell them that we're going to move Jack to another place and that we'll come over to pick him up personally." Gus nodded. "Then, I tell Bruce that the Newport people called and want him to come get Jack, that he's become unstable, too much to handle, etc."

"I'm with you," Gus said. "So he picks Jack up and drives him back through the Mojave. What if he wants you to go with him again?"

"Oh, I'll be so sick, so hungover, just can't get in the car, man." Greg put a sickly expression on his face.

Gus still wanted to make Greg say exactly what he wanted. "Where do I come in?"

"Well, like we talked about earlier, with your…skills, you could cause them to have an accident on the way back, if you know what I mean."

"Spell it out for me, Greg."

"I want you to hit the limo, make it explode, roll over, whatever," and Greg reached for the bag, "and here's fifty grand to make it happen, the sooner the better."

Gus let out a low whistle. "I can do that, but I don't think fifty grand is enough for killing three people. Remember you got the limo driver, too."

"Oh, believe me, I know. I have just the driver picked out for this trip." He smiled cruelly thinking of the driver who had been rude to him on their trip to deposit Jack in Newport in the first place. "What do they call it in war? Collateral damage? That's just what he would be, collateral damage."

"Getting back to the money…" Gus felt the weight of the bag and his heart rate accelerating. "I think you need to kick in another twenty five."

"Okay, no problem. When can you do it?" Greg agreed so easily that Gus felt like kicking himself, but even so it was a lot of money.

"I'd have to take a drive out there, scope it out," the sniper said thoughtfully. "It would be good to get the limo on a downhill stretch. Those things weigh a ton so the momentum would make it more of a crash." He tapped his fingernail on the side of his glass. "I'll go out there tomorrow and look around."

"So, it's a deal?"

"It's a deal, buddy." Gus put his hand out to shake Greg's. "I'll call you when I get back in town, let you know what I think. You work on what you're going to say to your jerk-off partner to get him in that limo."

Greg already had a script in mind but he didn't want to set things in motion until he was sure Gus was on board with the plan.

Jack listened, growing more amazed at Greg's willingness to kill his partner, to say nothing of killing him. Newport Shores was no longer safe, that much was certain. He had to alert the administrator to the possible call she was about to receive, and then he had a dozen other details to attend to. He also had a moral dilemma. Would he let the plot go forward, possibly killing Bruce and the limo driver, or would he stop it, turn the surveillance tapes over to the Las Vegas police and let them arrest Greg and Gus, then go after Bruce for the skimming? He walked over to the balcony off his living room. The marine layer felt calming and cool. He stood there thinking until it burned off and he had to retreat to his room. There was another matter he couldn't put off dealing with much longer. Hank. He had to make it right with the young man who had become so important to him.

Chapter Fifty-Five

Gus found the vantage point he needed, about a hundred yards off the highway, hidden by a small rock outcropping that gave him good visibility but also good protection. He would come out a night or two before the arranged date to bury the rifle then rebury it after he completed the job. He made a mental note to put a small camp shovel in his pickup truck. He could return later when any investigation concluded to unearth his prized long gun. He planned to leave his pickup truck in Primm, a few miles down the road, and it wouldn't do for passing drivers to see a man walking down the freeway with a rifle over his shoulder.

"Hey, it's all cool," he told Greg later. "I found a good spot, should be a piece of cake." They talked about the timing. "I've got something to do tomorrow, but Friday would work." Greg agreed that would give him enough time to make the call to Newport and get Bruce set up to go. "So, I guess Friday night you'll be celebrating."

"You've got that right. We get rid of Bruce and Jack on Friday, I'll stick around to look appropriately concerned, and the following week I'm off to a beach in Mexico."

"Well, I'll miss hanging out at Eroe with you," Gus said, thinking mostly of all the free drinks and food. "Mexico's cool. Find a friendly senorita and kick back."

"You should go, too," Greg said excitedly. Gus didn't really like talking on the phone about the whole arrangement and agreed to come by the casino later.

Jack heard them mention Friday and realized he had to get a plan in motion soon. It was time to make the call he had been dreading in one respect and looking forward to in another. He called Hank's cell phone number and was surprised to hear his answer. "Phoenix Aircraft, Hank speaking."

"Hank, it's Jack."

A long silence followed. "Jack, so...how are you? Long time no speak."

"I know, it's my fault."

"It sure is. I tried to call you at the casino but they wouldn't put me through."

"They wouldn't put anyone through, not just you, Hank."

"Yeah, and then my mom told me she saw you out at some nursing home she works at in Pahrump before you went back to the casino." Hank was working up a head of steam, clearly.

"Yes, I met your mom," Jack said quietly. "She's a very nice woman who seemed to care about the patients there. She was very good with them."

"Yeah, well, I'm not talkin' to her either."

"Listen, Hank, I need your help, and I'll explain everything." Hank didn't jump in to agree to Jack's request, but Jack persisted. "Some bad things are going down and I need you to come pick me up in Newport Beach, tomorrow if you can, but no later than Friday morning. Will you do that for me…please?"

Hank sighed. "Yeah, I'll be there. Tell me where." They finalized the details. "Do I need to bring the truck? Are you in a wheelchair still?"

"No, I'm back to normal, if you could call it that. Bring the Corvette." Before disconnecting Jack told Hank. "I really appreciate this, and I'm going to explain everything on the drive home."

"Whatever." Hank had his pride, too.

Greg was busy on the phone, too. "Could I speak to the administrator, Ms. Kelly? This is Greg Nelson calling from Las Vegas." The receptionist at Newport Shores put the call through to the administrator, who had been expecting it after hearing from Jack about the duo in Vegas had planned.

"Yes, Mr. Nelson. How can I help you?"

"Well, we have decided that Mr. Hamilton would be better placed in a different facility, and we would like to plan on picking him up Friday afternoon." Greg expected a fight, but the administrator readily agreed and said they would have Mr. Hamilton ready by noon. She wasted no time getting off the phone and went straight to Jack's room.

"It's set for Friday. They're coming to pick you up then, just as you thought." She took Jack's hand. "We've come to care about you here, and I can't help but be worried about what these characters might do."

"Not to worry, it's all under control," Jack assured her. "There is one more favor you might do for me though."

"Anything."

"I have a friend whose mother might be needing a job pretty soon. She works for those clods out in Pahrump, but I don't think their facility is going to be open much longer." Jack continued, "I don't know if she'd even come down here, but I'd like to leave her name with you, and if she does…"

"We would give her every consideration, of course," the administrator said.

"I'd actually pay her salary, if it comes to that," Jack volunteered, "but I think she'd earn it and you'd come to value her." He stood up to dismiss the administrator. "Now, I've got some other calls to make, if you don't mind." She left and Jack immediately got on the phone to the chief of security at Eroe, who was very surprised to hear him speaking. There was one detail about Friday's plan that bothered him, and that was the limo driver.

"Mr. Hamilton! How wonderful to hear your voice. I guess that stint by the ocean worked wonders," the security man said sincerely.

"Well, yes it did, and I'll be back at Eroe pretty soon, but keep that between you and me, okay?"

"Absolutely sir."

"Listen, have you gotten a request from Greg Nelson or Bruce Barnes for a limo for Friday?"

"Yes, just got it a few minutes ago. Mr. Nelson requested a stretch and a particular driver, uh, let's see, he wanted Brock Evans."

"So, what do you know about this guy? Brock?"

"He's a good driver, never scratched even the biggest stretch, but..."

"But, what?"

"He's kind of a bad character, sir. I know he's had several domestic calls out to his house for beating his wife. He's got girlfriends on the side who come here looking for him, and they look pretty questionable." The chief was clearly uncomfortable. "And, the biggest thing is we had a complaint from a female guest that he attempted to rape her in the limo coming from the airport."

"And you didn't fire him then?" Jack was incredulous.

"The HR department wouldn't let us, and the woman dropped her complaint, so it was out of my hands. But this is not a good guy."

"Okay, that's about what I need to know." Jack paused. "Be sure he gets that run on Friday then. I'll talk to you soon."

Greg still had to put the second part of his plan into action and roamed through the casino looking for Bruce, expecting to find him in his usual place in the counting room. Security had to scan anyone coming into the room and Greg was annoyed that his entry was rejected, but he waved at Bruce through the window, and after a few minutes Bruce came out.

"Listen, I just got a call from that cold-assed broad at Newport Shores. We've gotta go pick Jack up. They can't deal with him anymore."

"What's to deal with? He just sits there like a zombie." Bruce turned to go back to the counting room.

"No, I guess he just went berserk and was attacking the other patients, and they just said they can't keep him. They want him out by noon on Friday." Greg had to fight to keep the smile off his face. "And they said you personally have to come get him, you being his custodian and all."

"Oh crap! What the hell are we supposed to do with a berserk mental patient?" Bruce was definitely short-tempered normally but this pushed him right to the edge in sixty seconds.

Greg stood by looking helpless. "I guess I could call them and see if they could, you know, really dope him up for the ride and then we could put him back out in Pahrump."

"Yeah. I guess. Look, just deal with it." Bruce waved to someone in the adjacent casino cage. "I'll see you down in the garage Friday morning.

No you won't, Greg thought. You won't see me again.

Chapter Fifty-Six

Their first meeting was awkward. It reminded Jack of the many mornings he would pick Hank up by the road side and have to essentially start all over again with the young man. Hank climbed out of the 'Vette and Jack could see that he had added a little more muscle on his lanky frame. They shook hands tentatively, but then Jack hugged him, something he'd never done, and Hank didn't pull away. Things were going to be okay between them, Jack thought with satisfaction.

Hank tossed the keys to Jack who caught them easily with his new hook. "You drive. I'm bushed from drivin' down here." Jack had spent the morning on his computer, checking to see that the skimmed money was still in Greg's account, so that in addition to homicide charges, there would also be embezzlement and whatever else the prosecutors could come up with. He had also sent his copies of the surveillance of Greg and Gus to the Las Vegas Police Department.

"So, tell me everything," Jack began. "You're building the plane again, it sounds like?"

"Yeah, but let's start with what happened to our plane in the first place."

Jack dreaded revealing how stupid he had been, but Hank deserved his honesty. "When they brought it back from the simulator I got in it to drive it back into the hangar, then I took it for a spin down the landing strip." He exhaled heavily. "Then I took it up in the air."

"You flew it! You're not a pilot!"

"Well, I pretty well proved that," Jack admitted. "Actually, I flew it pretty good, but it hit an updraft and I panicked, pulled back on the wheel and sent it into a stall."

"How'd you get it out?"

"I didn't. I crashed about fifty or so miles out in the desert, demolished the plane, broke a couple ribs and my ankle. I ended up crawling for a day or more until I finally found a road and some rock hounds picked me up, took me to a hospital in Vegas."

"Why didn't you call me then?" Hank demanded.

"I was too ashamed. That's the truth." Jack concentrated on the heavy freeway traffic for a minute. "I didn't talk to anyone and finally these vultures from the nursing home in Pahrump picked me up and took me out there. That's when I met your mom."

"You could've called me, or she could've," Hank said in a surly tone.

"She didn't know anything about me or who I was. I still wasn't talking. I just wanted to crawl in a hole and that's pretty much what that place in Pahrump was. But then they found out who I am and right away they knew they had the goose that lays the golden egg, I guess." He explained about the gaming commission and the legal work Bruce and Greg went through to obtain control of Jack, and ultimately of Eroe.

"Damn. Those guys were weasels but they were smart ones, you gotta say that."

"Oh, yeah, very smart." He revealed to Hank about how he was able to keep tabs on them through the surveillance system, both while he was at Eroe and then remotely in Newport. "That's when the plot thickened, as they say."

"So now the one partner is planning to kill you and his partner? Wow. Straight outa television." Hank was clearly impressed.

Jack and Hank were about two hundred miles out of Newport Beach heading back to Las Vegas when Bruce pulled into the Newport nursing home. He was furious at Greg for not showing up earlier and insisting he was too hungover and too sick to his stomach to tolerate the long car ride. The limo pulled into the elaborate circular drive, coming to a stop in the porte cochere. Bruce waited imperiously for the driver to open his door, which he took his time doing. "Sir?" Bruce thought, "Two can play this game," and he refused to even acknowledge the driver. He went straight into the facility and directly to the administrator's office, not even waiting for the receptionist to announce his arrival.

"So, where is he?" Bruce demanded of the woman. "I thought you said he'd be ready to go."

"Oh, Mr. Barnes, so sorry you had to come all the way down here this morning. It seems there has been a change in plans."

Bruce looked at her, ready to explode. "Now you're keeping him?"

"No, not at all. His condition deteriorated so rapidly we were forced to send him to an acute psychiatric unit up in Los Angeles."

"So now I have to go there to get him?" Bruce was red in the face.

"I'm sorry, but I don't think Mr. Hamilton will be going anywhere for quite a while." She gave Bruce an icy smile. "It appears you've had a long ride for nothing today."

"You've never heard of a cell phone lady?" Bruce stormed out of her office and didn't wait for the limo driver to open his door. "Let's get the hell out of here."

Gus left his pickup in Primm early in the morning and walked through the desert to the rock formation where he had left the rifle the night before. He had a rolled-up blanket with him, something to make his wait on the desert floor a little more comfortable. He calculated the limo would be coming down the long straight-away into Primm around three o'clock.

Hank had thought Jack might want to go to the hangar to see the progress on the new plane. He told Jack about the arrangements he had made with the simulator company owner and worried Jack might object to the new partnership, but Jack relieved his worries. "It's exactly what I wanted you to do, take the reins on this thing." He smiled, "You might say I wanted you to just fly with it." As an afterthought, "You should take flying lessons. Those ten minutes were about the most exciting in my life." But instead of going to the hangar, Jack asked that they go to Primm instead, directing him to one of the three hotels there. "Go in and get a room, has to be west-facing and as high up as you can. When you get it, come out and get me." While Hank went in to make the arrangements, Jack rummaged around behind the seats and came up with a baseball cap. It wasn't perfect, but it would do.

Hank was back in a few minutes and gave him the room key. "Want me to come in?"

"No, you can get back to work, but come get me in the morning, about eight?"

Hank thought it was strange, but then everything in the last few months had been strange. "See you then."

Jack pulled the cap down low and walked quickly through the casino to the elevators, noting with satisfaction that the room was on the top floor. He figured he had about two hours to wait.

There were other limos, of course, flying down I-15 transporting gamblers to Las Vegas, but none with the distinctive lavender halogen lights and gray body color. Gus knew he wouldn't have any problem acquiring the target. As he lay there waiting a rattlesnake sidled up fairly close, seeming to take a look at Gus and then deciding to move on. He laughed. Professional courtesy, I guess. He finally saw the limo top the grade and start its descent into the Primm valley. He steadied the rifle's position on the rocks and slowed his breathing and heart rate, just as he had been trained to in the army.

When the limo was exactly in position, Gus shot out the right front tire, then seconds later the right rear. He was gratified there were no other cars immediately adjacent. The behemoth limo swerved gently at first, then twisted more violently and Gus could see the driver hopelessly fighting for control. The limo left the roadway and sailed over a berm just enough to send it airborne. When it came down, it came down nose-first. The explosion was deafening even at Gus's distance. The limo seemed to bounce on its nose, then somersaulted. Just to be on the safe side, Gus put another bullet into the exposed gas tank. Flames engulfed the car which continued to roll through the desert, finally coming to a rest on its side.

Satisfied, Gus used the blanket to wrap up the gun and buried it in the hole he had dug the previous night. He'd call Greg when he got to Primm.

Jack watched the fireball erupt out in the desert and tapped the window with his hook. Maybe all the 'kill' hadn't gone out of him after all.

Chapter Fifty-Seven

Jack stayed at the window for a long time. He watched the flames die down and saw the speeding California Highway Patrol cars head for the site, followed closely by a fire truck. He knew they'd find very little left of the limousine and after a cursory inspection would conclude that the driver may have fallen asleep or been distracted when he drifted off the road. The limo's speed and weight would have combined to launch it quite a ways away from the freeway.

He was lost in thought about having actually allowed the deaths of two men, although he didn't actually kill them himself. Perhaps two hours had passed when he looked out at the desert and saw a lone man walking toward Primm. That would be Gus, Jack speculated, and after another half-hour it became clear that it was indeed, Jack being able to see his flak jacket and recognized his characteristic loping gait. Jack called the head of security at Eroe. "Hey, it's Jack Hamilton. I need a favor."

"Anything. You name it."

"I want you to call security here at Pete's in Primm and ask them to escort me out to the parking lot in just a few minutes, and in the meantime, you call the Clark County Sheriff's office and have them get out here on the double." If the security chief wondered what was going on, he didn't ask and simply told Jack he'd get right on it. Minutes later there was a knock on the door and two security guards asked Jack's name and said they were there to do as he requested.

"Did you guys see the explosion out in the desert a couple hours ago?" Jack asked.

"That was something, all right," the one guard said although the other said he had been on the casino floor. Patrons who came in told him about it though.

"Well, the guy that caused it is going to be walking into your parking lot any minute." They couldn't help but look questioning. "Trust me. I know. I want you to stay with me when I meet him and detain him until the sheriffs arrive." He explained that he had already alerted them and they should be arriving about the same time. The two men squared their shoulders and walked Jack to the elevators. Jack pulled his borrowed baseball cap down tightly as they stepped into the parking lot. He saw Gus head for a banged-up Toyota, and drop something in the truck bed. When his back was turned, Jack tapped him on the shoulder with his hook. "Surprise."

Gus knew immediately who he was and began to stammer. "Hey, I didn't know…" The two burly guards each grabbed one of his arms and at that moment the sheriff's cruiser pulled into the lot. The officer got out with his weapon drawn, but the guards indicated Gus wasn't armed. The sheriff handcuffed him and put him in the back of the car.

"We're going to need to talk to you about this," the sheriff told Jack. "I can send another car out to take you back to Vegas."

"No, I'm planning on being there in the morning and I'll come straight to your offices." He paused. "I'll bring with me all the information you'll need to keep him locked up." It was all highly irregular but the sheriff knew the Eroe security chief who had already told him that Jack was a straight-shooter. As an afterthought. "There were no survivors from the crash?"

"We don't even know how many people were in the car. I don't think they've even got a license plate yet or any ID. What a frickin' mess." The sheriff scratched his head. "We get a drifter every month or so, they fall asleep or whatever and just drift off the road."

The security guards walked Jack back up to his room. He ordered a light meal from room service and then spent another hour on the phone with Eroe security, this time with their surveillance specialist. Jack told the man exactly which camera feeds contained the meeting between Greg and Gus in which they discussed killing Bruce and himself. He asked the specialist to make duplicate copies of the meeting to present to the sheriff's department the next morning. He also requested that all of the recent footage of Bruce in the counting room be compiled. There was someone dirty in that room and Jack would have to find out who.

He also had to find out how to get Eroe's money out of Greg's account and back into Eroe's coffers. The casino had perhaps a dozen accountants on staff, however, Jack realized, so that would be a relatively simple task for them. Until Greg was firmly in custody, however, Jack wanted the money left in the account to help bolster the case against him. Greg would certainly claim that Bruce had skimmed the money, which was true, to a point. Greg also clearly hadn't planned on giving it back.

Jack was exhausted when he finally got off the phone. He doubted he'd be able to sleep but was pleasantly surprised when the sun poked through the curtains. He would just have enough time to shower and have a small breakfast before Hank arrived. He wondered what Hank was feeling about his return—probably a little apprehensive and, no doubt, still a little angry.

Chapter Fifty-Eight

Greg pounded down one shot after the next, nervously checking his cell phone every few minutes. He couldn't understand why Gus hadn't called or come by Eroe, but he was fairly certain the deed had been done successfully because he had seen no sight of Bruce all night. Finally, near midnight, the bartender cut Greg off and called security to take him to his suite.

The next morning Hank was right on time to pick up Jack and started to make the turn out of the parking lot leading to the Mojave and the hangar, but Jack stopped him. "No, we need to go to Vegas first." Jack could feel Hank's frustration begin to bubble up that quickly. "You heard about the explosion yesterday didn't you?"

"Yeah, so they did it, huh?"

"They certainly did and now I need to go to Vegas to tie up some loose ends. You can hang out with me or you can sit by the pool."

Hank seemed to consider it but said nothing either way and they rode the forty miles to Las Vegas in silence. Jack directed Hank to a garage entrance only for casino executives at Eroe, and Hank was clearly impressed by how quickly the garage staff ran to greet Jack. The security head was there and mumbled a few words to Jack, ending with, "He's in his suite, if that's where you want it to go down." Jack nodded and turned back to signal Hank to follow along.

A sheriff's deputy was waiting for them outside the door to Greg's suite. The Eroe security man used a pass key to open the door and all four men entered the suite, a much smaller version of Jack's but still quite elegant. The picture Greg presented was less so. He was still dressed from the night before, passed out face up on the bed; he had clearly vomited at some point during the night. As the others looked on in disgust, Jack leaned close, nearly gagging on the sour whiskey sweat and vomit smell. He thumped Greg's sternum quite hard. He woke up to see Jack standing over him. "What? Shit man."

"So, does this creep you out a little, Greg?" Jack stepped a few feet back. "I imagine the boys in prison will creep you out a little more." He turned to the deputy. "He's all yours." The deputy pulled on rubber gloves, rolled Greg over roughly and cuffed him. He'd read him his rights in the elevator. The others exited Greg's suite and Jack indicated he'd like to go up to his own for a change of clothing. The security chief turned beet red.

"Actually, sir, you can't," he began. "Someone else is staying there." Jack glared at him. "It was Mr. Barnes' idea to rent it out to the high-rollers."

"Well, Mr. Barnes is no longer in our employ. Get hold of the front desk and get them out of my suite." He laughed. "Put them here in Greg's place. He won't be needing it." The security man was already on his phone.

Jack grabbed Hank by the shoulder. "Okay, one more stop at the sheriff's office and we're out of here, unless you want to stay here, hang out." Hank was clearly intimated by Eroe's luxury and just followed Jack to the elevator leading back down to the private garage.

When they got to the sheriff's office Jack realized he would have to go out in public and hesitated, but after all, he'd been through so much worse lately, a few stares weren't likely to do him in. They passed through security, no mean feat considering Jack's prosthetic leg and the threatening-looking hook, but eventually reached a receptionist. "Sheriff Delaney is expecting me. Jack Hamilton." She jumped up briskly and led them down a long hall to an office that was nearly as large as Jack's suite at Eroe. The sheriff was standing when Jack and Hank entered and immediately shook hands with both.

"'Mr. Hamilton, thank you for coming in." He offered them coffee which they both declined. "We have all the security footage you sent in, and we've already met with the LVPD about their end of this…situation." He looked like he didn't know what to say next. "We're uncertain, I guess you might say, about why you didn't take steps to prevent the, uh, accident yesterday."

Jack had anticipated this question. "Well, to be honest, I didn't think they had the balls to actually do it. I mean, sir, as a precaution I did get out of Newport Beach and I would not have gotten in that limo, but truly, I never expected it to really happen." He looked as sincere as he did when acting in *The Corner Saloon*.

"Well, we brought Mr. Nelson, Greg Nelson, is it, into custody this morning, and we've had his associate, Gus Jacobs, in a holding area since last night. Is there anyone else that's involved?"

Jack thought about the counting room and the skim but thought that would be better handled internally at Eroe. "No, I think that about covers it." Clearing his throat, Jack asked, "How are you going to play this in the media?"

"I don't know if I fully appreciate your question, Mr. Hamilton."

"It's just that if the media get wind of a plot to kill me and steal money from the casino, it's like the bad old so-called mob days all over again."

"I see where they would get that impression."

"We run a clean house at Eroe, always have. These were just three penny ante crooks, really. I'd like to see it just put out as two employees of Eroe being in a car accident and leave it at that." Jack thought one of the sharper news editors might very well make the connection between Greg no longer being at the hotel and Bruce being dead, but he couldn't worry about that. He gave the sheriff his cell phone number and a direct line at Eroe, then thanked him for his time.

"Okay, Hank, one more stop and we're outta here." Hank looked relieved. He directed Hank to the Nevada Bank on Fremont. Rather than going to a teller's window, he approached one of the bank officers at her desk. "I'd like to see the bank manager, if I may? I'm Jack Hamilton, president of Eroe." She was too preoccupied with how he looked to really have listened to him, so he was forced to repeat himself. "It's an urgent matter, please."

She left her desk and came back a few moments later with a middle-aged man who introduced himself as James Wilson. "What can I do for you gentlemen?" He was nearly salivating at the thought of getting Eroe as a customer.

"Actually, I just wanted to alert you that Eroe will be making a substantial withdrawal from one of your accounts, that account being in the name of Greg Nelson."

"Nelson?" He used the bank officer's computer to pull up the account. "Perhaps we better step into my office," he said quietly. They followed him into a rather ordinary office. "That account has several million dollars in it."

"Yes, but it's several million dollars stolen illegally from Eroe." Jack knew the manager's distress. "I just came as a courtesy to let you know that our accountants and the federal prosecutor will be in shortly to start the process." He leaned forward. "Naturally, they'll appreciate your cooperation." The bank manager looked ill but said he would do everything necessary to assist them.

They walked out into the bright sunshine. "You know, Hank, it's all a house of cards. With Greg locked up and Bruce dead, your mom's going to be out of a job, too." Hank looked questioning. "That federal prosecutor is going to close Pahrump Place, probably as soon as they can get the patients moved to other facilities."

"Yeah, I guess so."

"So, I think on the way to the hangar we need to go to Pahrump and pick up your mom."

"I don't want nothin' to do with her. I'm still mad at her for lying to me about you," Hank said defiantly.

Jack expected this, too. "I think she was just looking out for you." They climbed into Hank's truck and Jack said no more on the subject until they were on the freeway. "You know, it's very hard sometimes to understand why people do the things they do." Hank wouldn't even look at him. "I know you don't understand what I did either, but maybe someday you will. But here's the thing. Any mother always wants what's best for their children, and that's what your mom wanted. She could see how well you were doing with the airplane and she wanted your success," and he hesitated, "and your happiness to continue."

"Well, she had a damn funny way of going about it," Hank snapped. "And so did you!"

"I know. That's just what I was saying." They drove a few more miles. "Okay, we won't go see her right now. They'll probably need her, as it is, to help get all the patients out of that dump."

"So, we finally going to the hangar?"

"Yep. I can't wait."

Chapter Fifty-Nine

When Hank turned off the freeway onto the road that eventually led to the hangar, he began laughing uncontrollably, startling Jack out of his own thoughts. "You know what I just thought of?" He could hardly get the words out for laughing. "Since Bruce and that other guy don't have custody of you anymore, you could become a foster child?" He howled with laughter. "Yeah, I can see that. 'Course you're so ugly probably nobody'd adopt you."

Jack couldn't help but laugh just to see Hank laughing, but he still thought, strange kid. Hank had been like this from day one of their relationship, of course, one day open and talkative, the next completely closed off. "You do know how weird you are, don't you?" He jabbed Hank in the ribs with his hook.

"Ha! You should know what weird is I guess." Hank stopped laughing when they pulled up to the hangar and saw a semi truck waiting out front. "They weren't supposed to be here until tomorrow." He shut the motor off and went to speak to the trucker while Jack stayed in the truck, thankful for the darkened windows, although he rolled one down just a little in order to hear the conversation.

"You're going to have to pull around the other direction and then back it in, right up to the hangar door," he told the driver who looked reluctant but climbed back in the cabin and did as Hank directed while Hank opened the hangar doors. Jack was astounded at what he saw. In the time Hank had waited for Jack's return apparently he did nothing but clean and organize the shop in the hangar. It looked like a surgical suite in its precision. The central work table where they had done all their planning and which had taken up a quarter of the space had been replaced by a drop-down drafting table of sorts, freeing up enough room for a second airplane chassis.

Hank supervised the unloading of the fiberglass for the planes. Gone was the red, white and blue design and in its place was a lustrous gold darkening to a deep orange with a dramatic black Phoenix bird in the center of the fuselage. The leading edges of the wings had a flame design which made Jack shudder but he could appreciate the symbolism and the design. It was even more beautiful than their first prototype.

When the driver pulled away, Jack got out and walked to the pile of fiberglass sheets. "It's just beautiful," he said, running his hand along one of the wings. "Who came up with the design?"

"Oh, my partner did. Oh wait, just a minute, I don't have a partner, he's too busy fooling around in a casino" Hank said, still evidently in a playful mood. "I came up with it. Figured it made sense."

"It more than makes sense." Jack couldn't take his eyes off it. The phone rang, giving him time to sort out his emotions.

"Phoenix Aircraft, Hank speaking." Jack listened to Hank negotiate the price and delivery dates for a series of parts for the motors, a job that had fallen to Jack in the past. When that call ended, two more came in and Jack listened with pride at how competently—and confidently—Hank handled each one.

"Whew, some days are crazy." Hank told Jack about how helpful Mr. Shelburn, the owner of the flight simulator had been and about their plans for Hank to finish these two planes, sending one to East coast airshows and keeping the other out West. But then Hank's enthusiasm seemed to ebb. "Of course, now that you're back, you probably have different ideas about the whole thing."

Jack was still almost too emotional to speak. It turns out his finest accomplishment had been Hank. Before his eyes the gawky loner he had picked up in the desert a year ago had become more than an able assistant or a glorified gofer. He was the head of his own company, an exceptional designer, and clearly a take-charge executive. "Well, the only idea I have is that when you get your pilot's license, you take me up in one of these beauties." He still couldn't look Hank in the eye and just walked around the chassis and the fiberglass. "I think I'm about done with the airplane business."

"You're still going to be here, aren't you?" Hank seemed a little anxious.

"Oh, I'll come by, see how you're doing, but you've got it under control. You don't need me getting in the way, and I'm sure as hell not going to be your parts runner." Both men laughed.

"Yeah, I can't see you snaggin' a bag of burgers and two shakes with that hook of yours," Hank grinned.

"Oh, I don't know about that. You might be surprised." The banter seemed forced.

"So, what are you going to do, go back to the casino?"

"I don't think so. The board pretty much runs things. I don't blame them for how they used Bruce in my place." Jack had thought about the issue a great deal. In truth, the board's actions had allowed the casino to expand to another, even bigger property, something that might not have happened had Jack been around and unwilling to appear before the gaming commission. "I think I'll let them just keep the money rolling in. I might even let loose of my suite there."

Jack hadn't really made a plan for his life until that moment. He couldn't help but think of how relaxed he felt in Newport Beach. The morning marine layer along the coast was cool and calming, something Las Vegas would never be. He might just hire Scottie, his former assistant from Newport Shores. That would create a job opening for Hank's mom if she wanted it. Jack could look for a nice piece of land with a view of the ocean. He'd build the house he had imagined with the big loggia where he could spend his afternoons thinking of the next big thing.

The End

About the Author

Arline Fisher was raised in Carson City, Nevada, and is a journalism graduate from the University of Nevada, Reno. She has been the managing editor of several regional and national magazines and has worked in direct-mail marketing and public relations. She recently published *The Corner Saloon*. She makes her home in St. George, Utah.

Thank you for your support

I have enjoyed the endless support of my friends, notably those who were willing to read a chapter nearly every day and offer their comments and encouragement: Vicki Lund, Claudia Reek, Lonna Burress, Kirsten Ball and Lolly Seal. Janet Rodenkirch and Rudi Francis earned my appreciation for their comments and, in Rudi's case, her insight about cover design. My thanks also goes to Ron Vogel whose stories about being in the Navy inspired me to cast Jack as a soldier, and to Jim Rodenkirch, another Navy Chief, who helped me refine my descriptions of life on a destroyer.

Thanks also to authors Sheldon Siegel and J. Carson Black who generously shared their insights into the world of publishing today and encouraged me greatly.

My biggest thanks goes to my Aunt Arline Bogle without whom none of this would have been possible. I wish she was still here to read my work and to share her wry sense of humor.

If you've enjoyed what you read in KEEPER, please write a favorable review, tell your friends, and send me an e-mail at arlinefisher@centurylink.net.

Publisher: Arline Fisher
arlinefisher@centurylink.net

Copyright @ Arline Fisher, 2015

Publisher's Note: This is a work of fiction. Names, characters, places and incidents either are the product of the author's imagination or are used fictitiously, and any resemblance to actual persons, living or dead, businesses, or locales is entirely coincidental.

ISBN-13:978-0692586259
ISBN-10:0692586253

All rights reserved. No part of this publication may be reproduced, stored in or introduced into a retrieval system, or transmitted in any form or by any means (electronic, mechanical, by photocopying, recording or otherwise) without the prior written permission of the publisher/author. Please respect the author's rights and purchase only authorized printed or electronic editions.

www.ingramcontent.com/pod-product-compliance
Lightning Source LLC
Chambersburg PA
CBHW061425040426
42450CB00007B/899